On any given week, pastors receive a cacophony of promotions on how to be on the cutting edge of ministry—conferences on leadership and the latest creative way to do ministry, books on vision and ways to implement it. All good materials! How refreshing, however, to receive the practical and pointed material from London and Wiseman! By focusing on five vital areas in every pastor's life, the authors offer a basic and essential foundation for *being* an authentic minister, not just *doing* ministry. Job 4:4 reads, "Your words have put stumbling people on their feet" (*THE MESSAGE*). So does *The Shepherd's Covenant for Pastors*. Don't even think of going on to other important ministry components until you've embraced this message.

DR. PAUL S. HONTZ
Central Wesleyan Church
Holland, Michigan

Periodically a book comes along that captures the heart of a pastor, especially if deep in the recesses of that pastor's heart he desires to go the distance. The subject matter of this book is an absolute must-read for every pastor. I commend its reading if you really desire to finish well.

DR. JOHNNY M. HUNT
Senior Pastor, First Baptist Church
Woodstock, Georgia

The Shepherd's Covenant for Pastors should be required reading for every pastor who is dedicated to a lifelong pursuit of faithfulness and fruitfulness. I wholeheartedly recommend this book to you!

REV. WALT KALLESTAD
Senior Pastor, Community Church of Joy
Phoenix, Arizona

Dr. H. B. London has the heart of a pastor, and that is the greatest reason why we listen when he speaks to us. He's been there, done that, felt that and knows the everyday jolts and joys of the ministry. When I have faced very personal needs, I have called him and benefited from his wisdom. *The Shepherd's Covenant for Pastors* puts us face-to-face with the realities of ministry today. No one I know speaks better to those issues than H. B. London.

REV. DR. DANIEL MERCALDO
Senior Pastor and Founder, Gateway Cathedral
Staten Island, New York

H. B. London and Neil Wiseman know the heart and soul of the ministry. They identify, with deadly precision, the problems and obstacles every pastor faces. They provide simple and practical steps that anyone can follow to enhance one's personal relationship with God, one's family and the church.

BOB RUSSELL
Senior Minister, Southeast Christian Church
Louisville, Kentucky

I don't think there has ever been a time when pastors have been under more pressure than they are today. In a culture that is increasingly indifferent—if not downright hostile—to the gospel, pastors face enormous challenges that often sap their strength, undermine their confidence and threaten their capacity to minister effectively.

Staying alive spiritually is a crucial issue for every pastor, as is maintaining healthy relationships and a positive attitude toward others, especially to those whom one is called to minister.

The Shepherd's Covenant for Pastors gives helpful guidance to today's ministers of the gospel. Every pastor needs to read this book and apply it to his or her own life; it can help, and the Lord knows we need all the help we can get!

JOHN H. STEVENS
Pastor, First Presbyterian Church
Colorado Springs, Colorado

the shepherd's
covenant

FOR PASTORS

H. B. LONDON, Jr.
NEIL B. WISEMAN

Regal

From Gospel Light
Ventura, California, U.S.A.

PUBLISHED BY REGAL BOOKS
FROM GOSPEL LIGHT
VENTURA, CALIFORNIA, U.S.A.
PRINTED IN THE U.S.A.

Regal Books is a ministry of Gospel Light, a Christian publisher dedicated to serving the local church. We believe God's vision for Gospel Light is to provide church leaders with biblical, user-friendly materials that will help them evangelize, disciple and minister to children, youth and families.

It is our prayer that this Regal book will help you discover biblical truth for your own life and help you meet the needs of others. May God richly bless you.

For a free catalog of resources from Regal Books/Gospel Light, please call your Christian supplier or contact us at 1-800-4-GOSPEL *or* www.regalbooks.com.

Library of Congress Cataloging-in-Publication Data
London, H. B.
  The shepherd's covenant for pastors / H.B. London, Neil B. Wiseman.
      p. cm.
  Includes bibliographical references.
  ISBN 0-8307-3740-5 (hardcover)
  1. Pastoral theology. I. Wiseman, Neil B. II. Title.

  BV4011.3.L66 2005
  253—dc22   2005010024

2   3   4   5   6   7   8   9   10 / 15   14   13   12   11   10   09

Rights for publishing this book in other languages are contracted by Gospel Light Worldwide, the international nonprofit ministry of Gospel Light. Gospel Light Worldwide also provides publishing and technical assistance to international publishers dedicated to producing Sunday School and Vacation Bible School curricula and books in the languages of the world. For additional information, visit www.gospellightworldwide.org; write to Gospel Light Worldwide, P.O. Box 3875, Ventura, CA 93006; or send an e-mail to info@gospellightworldwide.org.

FOR BEVERLEY AND BONNIE,
WHO HAVE SHARED AND
AFFIRMED OUR JOURNEY.

CONTENTS

Part 3: A Servant-Shepherd's Heart

Part 4: Constant Safeguards

Part 5: Embrace God Intimately

ministry is all
about grace

*God is able to make all grace abound to you, so
that in all things at all times, having all that you need,
you will abound in every good work.*

2 CORINTHIANS 9:8

This book is about *grace*. Its theme is grace; its heartbeat
is grace.

It would be difficult to estimate how many times I
(H. B.) have uttered the words, "But by the grace of
God." He has blessed me, and probably you as well, with
what I've learned to call unmerited favor.

I've read many definitions and explanations of the
term "grace," but I firmly believe people must experience

grace if they're going to understand it even remotely. You've probably preached on grace from time to time, but have you ever considered the role of grace in your life and ministry?

People have always teased me by saying, "H. B., you're a trophy of amazing grace." I agree. I *am* a trophy of God's love and mercy—somewhat battered, dented and worn, but still His trophy. I can certainly relate to the words of that age-old, classic hymn by John Newton: "Amazing grace! how sweet the sound That saved [and protected] a wretch like me!"

I'll never forget a moment in my pastoral life when I learned that a colleague had failed morally. It staggered me. After the initial shock of his actions—which I took personally—I was angry. I wanted to tell him off, to let him have it, to give him a healthy dose of my judgment. As I was attempting to make that contact, a voice in my head whispered, "Be careful, Son; but for My grace that could be you." Immediately I retreated from my mission of condemnation to one of self-inspection—and I thanked my Lord for His reminder.

Each of us could put a paragraph in this book that would testify to God's grace. Think about it. Your conversion—miraculous! Your journey into ministry—amazing! God has used your meager gifts and talents to represent Him in many ways, and in each of those times you could step back and say, "But by the grace of God."

The last thing I want to appear is negative—especially when the theme is grace—but it's hard to believe that any one of us, regardless of how gifted or blessed we may be, might have the audacity for one moment to take pride in our accomplishments. I learned the hard way in my own journey to take my work and ministry seriously, but not take myself too seriously. I recall a time early in my pastoral career when I was having a certain degree of success and fell into the habit of reading my press clippings. As I look back on those times, I can see that this habit not only alienated me from my friends in the ministry but also affected my closeness with the Lord. In many ways, it seemed as if He was saying to me, "If you want to do ministry by yourself, then go ahead and try."

Of course, it's possible to have a measure of meaningful ministry without God's grace, but there will always be a hollowness to it. There will be an emptiness that only His grace can fill. That emptiness might almost be like accomplishing something of note, such as a hole-in-one or a spectacular stunt on a bike or surfboard, but not having anyone to share it with. We need Someone to fill the emptiness and make our lives more trusting than striving.

A huge danger lurks in the church today. It is characterized by a mind-set that spotlights the person rather than the God who called us. For pastors, popularity, prestige and power are as addictive as any drug— and so, we must avoid this drug and the high it brings.

How then do we maintain a balance in our call that adequately reflects our contribution and God's grace at the same time? Well, that's what the book is about—balance. Balance personifies the ultimate in ministry. How do we maintain balance when the calls to serve both God and people collide? What do we do when the responsibilities of the church take precedence over our family? How do we change direction when the work of the church becomes more alluring than intimacy with the Lord?

When faced with decisions that carry major consequences, which road will we take? The road most dangerous and fleeting? Or the road that leads to the applause of our Lord? So many of our colleagues have missed the gift of grace called balance because their mind-set and aptitude fell victim to the enchantment of the world.

Yet His grace is sufficient (see 2 Cor. 12:9). God looks at our arrogance, yet He loves us like a father loves his child. The Lord sees our faults, but He envisions us as holy. He sees when we've hurt Him by our selfishness and our prideful ways, yet He patiently waits for the right moment to slip His arms around us and say, "I love you, My son, My daughter. Please don't destroy your effectiveness."

Most of all, when we sin, when we fall short, when our ways are not His ways, when rebellion gets the upper hand, He pursues us because He knows that's when we need Him most. Now that's grace! He could walk away and be done with us, but He doesn't. He could turn His attention to a more gifted and talented child, but He doesn't. He could take us out of the line-up, but He doesn't. He could say something like, "Why did I ever call you in the first place?" but He doesn't. He could even say something like, "Do you know how much you've hurt Me?" but He doesn't.

Instead, in His grace He makes His presence known. And like a gentle breeze or a soft kiss or a loving arm around our shoulder, He's there. That's grace.

I'm sure more scholarly and theologically sound defenses exist for grace, but I just know how grace works for me. I echo the truth expressed in Julia Johnston's classic hymn: "Grace, grace, God's grace, grace that is greater than all our sin!"[1]

H. B. London

authenticity is nourished by grace

This book is built on three Christ-exalting words. Two are found in the book's title, "shepherd" and "covenant," and the third is found in the basic outline of its contents, an acrostic built on the word "grace."

Shepherd, covenant, grace. This trio of words asks probing questions that reach deep within us and stretch our souls. They pierce our hearts and deal with who we are and how God set us apart for the ministry.

Shepherd, covenant, grace. These three words, when applied to the practice of ministry, test our motive, challenge our commitment, energize our perseverance and evaluate our competence.

Shepherd, covenant, grace. These words together raise a warning, question a trend and encourage vigilance.

The warning: Many pastors are committing moral suicide—destroying churches, families, others and themselves. This disgrace and hemorrhage of talent has to stop.

The trend: Many pastors spend too much energy focusing on generality and trivia and trying to keep people happy, while neglecting the destruction that sin causes in their homes, their churches and their communities.

And the encouragement: Those three words—shepherd, covenant, grace—urge every minister of the gospel to become part of a growing movement of ministers who promise to God, their spouse, congregation and colleagues to maintain and enjoy a life of holiness and righteousness.

Grace—a Magnificently Free Gift from God

We're saved by grace. Kept by grace. Given sufficient grace to meet with gallant fortitude every demand, responsibility and surprise of our living. Behind it all is the extravagant initiative of God, expressed most obviously in His sending His Son as the Giver of grace.

Grace shows up on nearly every page of the New Testament. The apostle Paul opened every letter with a grace salutation and ended every letter with an affirming mention of the word. In writing to the churches, no matter how big the problem, how fervent the affirmation or how mind-stretching the theology, Paul started and ended with grace. He never could forget what grace did for him and what it can do for all who will receive it.

Like the apostle Paul, every pastor—and every believer—was first drawn to God by the faint stirring of grace. We were all saved by grace and maintain a life of holiness and righteousness by grace. Grace nourishes our ministry so that we are directed, empowered, protected and made effective. Grace was there from the start, and grace will take us home to God.

As if breaking into a spirited song or exhilarating poetry, William Barclay, the New Testament scholar of another era, wrote,

Grace is the power of God which clothes a person with day-to-day fortitude and strength.

Grace is that power of God which adorns a person's life with lovely things. Grace is a person's day-to-day defense and inspiration. Grace is not only the glory of the mountain top; it is the source of strength for the ordinary road of the everyday.[1]

Mark it down, preach it clearly, and rejoice with your whole being as you remember that grace—this undeserved generosity of God—is given and never earned. Grace is always adequate and inexhaustible and limitless and abundant. Grace is a kind of shorthand word for everything God is and does for us.[2] It's shorthand for all the nobility, beauty and opportunity He brings into our ministries.

Grace and Covenant Form a Love Connection

A covenant is a vow, a commitment, a determination to keep a promise. Think of the vows of marriage, responsibilities of citizenship or the pledge of government leaders to uphold the Constitution. Think of the ordination vows to be a faithful minister.

At first blush, vows and covenants sound like human efforts—merit and good works. Does that mean that grace requires some sort of obligation? How can grace be free, and yet the recipient of grace must commit to a life of holiness and righteousness? The answer is that such a commitment is our response to grace.

E. Stanley Jones, the sainted Methodist missionary-evangelist, explained the connection between grace and covenant like this:

> Grace binds us with far stronger cords than the cords of duty and obligation can bind us. Grace is free, but once you take it, you are bound forever to the Giver and bound to catch the Spirit of the Giver. Like produces like. Grace makes you gracious, the Giver makes you want to give.[3]

For generations, believers have been singing about this grace connection when they sing Isaac Watts' hymn "When I Survey the Wondrous Cross": "Love so amazing, so divine, demands my soul, my life, my all!"[4] The connection between covenant and grace is a love connection that starts with grace. And our response is to give our loving service to the One who gave us eternal life.

"Shepherd" Completes the Word Trio

Finally, we turn to shepherding. Grace draws us to ministry and keeps us there. Making a covenant is our loving response to grace and to the Giver of grace. Shepherding is one way we show our response to grace—it's the action of ministry motivated by the love of God we've received.

Of course, pastors don't have it easy these days. Yet think of the privilege—shepherding provides opportunities to deal with sin-wounded souls and then to challenge them with the grace of God. And again, grace is enough.

Shepherd, make a covenant to be nourished by grace.

a note to our readers

Caring for pastors, sharing with pastors and developing pastors comprise the heart commitment of the authors of this book. Nearly every page of this book deals with some phase of shepherding. We've authored 11 books together—all of them to support and encourage pastors.

As you begin to read, be aware that the message of *The Shepherd's Covenant for Pastors* may strike more deeply than that of some of our other books. Without apology, we've tried to aim it right at your heart—as if you're the only person who will ever read this book. However, we never mean to sound as if we're preaching at you—we humbly acknowledge that we're simply fellow shepherds, walking somewhere along the same path that you're following.

Having said that, we encourage you to note just a few things about the book's structure. It follows an acrostic that is built on the word "grace."

G   Genuine Accountability
R   Right Relationships
A   A Servant-Shepherd's Heart
C   Constant Safeguards
E   Embrace God Intimately

Those five phrases form the book's framework. Each of the five parts of the book corresponds to one of those phrases. In each part, you'll find a brief definition of the aspect of the Shepherd's Covenant that is being focused on in that part, a prayer that leads you into the heart of the topic, a story from a pastor whose life and ministry illustrate God's grace as it relates to that aspect of the covenant, and several chapters that explain the whys and practical how-tos for living out that commitment.

We'd like to add a special note about the pastor's stories that introduce each part of the book and the brief quotes that you'll find at the beginning of each chapter. Like our writing, much of our ministry involves coming alongside pastors—at Focus on the Family, in our work in pastors' gatherings, in personal conversations and in correspondence. Much of what we hear from pastors is personal, confidential and private. So while each story and note in this book is true, we've added color or altered details so that no one will guess whose story is being told. This allows us to present true-to-life stories of ministry without singling out anyone.

Also, if you have heard us speak or have read our writings, some of what you find in this book may sound somewhat familiar. That is because we have tried to bring timeless truth and the accumulation of our best thinking into the covenant described in this book.

We hope we've put together an easy-to-read, practical and inspirational book. Again, our goal is to equip you to understand and make this commitment to God, your family, your congregation and your colleagues. However, sometimes the things that hit closest to home aren't the easiest to read. We've deliberately kept the chapters in this book short. If you can't read the whole book or one of the five parts in one sitting, commit to reading a chapter a day. You'll be finished in less than a month, and your life and ministry will be nourished and strengthened in the process.

H. B. and Neil

the shepherd's
covenant

We are joined together by a common call of God to feed His sheep, but we are also tied by a common commitment to purity, holiness, righteousness and faithfulness. Our agreement to submit to the Shepherd's Covenant transcends theological differences, denominational connections and local congregational constraints. We are bound to one another by our calls, mutual accountability and by the knowledge that one day the Great Shepherd will be our final Judge.

We further believe that when clergy are more focused on mission than on profession, we will see a renewed interest in the churches we serve and a genuine acceptance by those we seek to influence. It is through God's grace that commitment to this covenant is made possible.

Genuine Accountability

Right Relationships

A Servant-Shepherd's Heart

Constant Safeguards

Embrace God Intimately

PART 1

grace

genuine
accountability

There is a great difference between being cordial and collegiate. We need colleagues in our lives who will ask us hard questions and allow us to do the same with them.

Jonathan became one in spirit with David,
and he loved him as himself.

1 SAMUEL 18:1

Holy Father,
Give me faith that makes my horizons reach to eternity
and beyond. Help me live in continuous contact with You—
so close that Your disciplines and directives make any plan
of human accountability seem easy. Save me from stupidities
and sins that shrivel the soul, torpedo influence and scar
memories forever. Keep me modest, clean and useful.
Amen

my soul
friend

Throughout the 20 years that I've been a pastor, I've usually resisted the idea of an accountability partner. The churches I've served have been in rural areas, where pastors still have a pretty prominent place in the community. That alone has helped me maintain a respectable lifestyle.

Things changed a couple of years ago when we moved to a suburban area near a large city. I love my church, so much so that I hope to retire here. It's not perfect, but it's pretty good. The church is growing, as the area around our facility booms with new houses, shopping areas and young families that are moving in.

This move put my family in a large city for the first time. The temptations are different here—if I chose to, I could drive 20 or 30 minutes in any direction and anonymously do pretty much anything I wanted to do. It scared me that those thoughts actually entered my mind—enough that I realized I needed to do something about it.

One of the draws of moving here was renewing a friendship with a seminary friend. Tom lives about a half hour away, where he serves a church in the inner city. During our seminary days, we often had heated discussions about theology and interpretations of Scripture. While we didn't always agree, we became good friends. To renew our friendship, we decided to meet every couple of weeks.

I never really considered my friendship with Tom to be an accountability relationship, but in the two years I've been at this church, our times together have already saved my ministry several times. While the people in my church will overlook some of my faults or not even be aware of them, Tom challenges me right when I need it. I'm certainly not on any pedestal in his eyes.

There have been a couple of times when I wanted to cancel a meeting with Tom. I remember one time when I'd been sick, I'd been caring for sick family members, and I was dealing with an ethical problem with one of our church lay leaders. I was pretty worn out. I e-mailed Tom and suggested that I could really use that half day to catch up with other things. But he must have read something between the lines that told him I really needed to spend the time with him. Tom wouldn't take no for an answer. Somewhat reluctantly, I confirmed the time and place we planned to meet.

When we got together, the Lord seemed to give Tom the right words to say and the right questions to ask me. Somehow, the discussion got to where we were talking about the dangers of running on fumes. Neither of us had all the answers, but we talked for over an hour about the importance of maintaining a strong spiritual walk even when family life and ministry seem to be burning us out.

After a time of very specific prayer about what we'd discussed, we both drove away encouraged and more prepared for the attacks that come from the enemy in times of weakness and discouragement.

I thank God for giving me a soul friend who knows me so well—and who knows our God well, too.

grace

develop
a great soul

*I'm discovering that when I read Scripture and spend
time praying for the people of my church, I feel closer
to God. It's like a spiritual guidance system—almost like
radar. I feel more aware of what God wants done,
when and sometimes even why.*

MATT, 35, FLORIDA

Oxygen is required for human life to exist.

Fuel is needed for an automobile to run.

And intimacy with Christ is the essential element
and necessary fuel for useful ministry.

If your faith doesn't show through your ministry,
you're simply an echo of what God intends you to be.
Your personal relationship with God greatly affects
everything in ministry.

As a spiritual leader, if you're not Christlike, you can't be productive. Jesus was absolutely correct when He warned, "If a man remains in me and I in him, he will bear much fruit; apart from me you can do nothing" (John 15:5). Note the promise—bearing much fruit.

Merely standing close to spiritual fires won't make your ministry vibrant. Without constant contact with Jesus, you'll soon become shallow, your vision superficial, your influence diluted and your satisfaction near zero. You'll be a pathetic imitation of the real thing.

To be genuinely productive, all of your ministry must integrate personal piety and painstaking intentional competence. One of the best ways to pursue personal holiness is to find someone who will hold you accountable in both spiritual and practical ways. But before you consider finding and empowering such a soul friend, first examine what you need to be held accountable to and why.

Getting into Spiritual Shape

It's easy to get out of shape spiritually. Once you've expended your spiritual stamina in long hours of preaching, teaching, counseling and performing other types of service, you have little reserve available to keep your own soul in shape.

It's a vicious cycle. When you try to function without spiritual energy, you feel perpetually spent and stressed. You fret over the inconsistency between what is and what ought to be. Just the momentum of ministry makes you dizzy and you grow bone weary. Without ever getting fired up, you burn out. And your ministry becomes a mere responsibility to fulfill or a frustrating job that can easily be cast off when the going gets tough.

Does all of this sound familiar? Every task requires too much effort. An accumulation of weariness corrodes your soul, sabotages your ministry and shatters your concept of self. Your ministry seems to be dying a slow, agonizing death, eventually to be buried under a tombstone marked with these words: "I died early because I tried to do it all on my own."

Getting into shape spiritually promises so much more. God desires that every aspect of your life and ministry be intricately woven around Christ. Vibrant ministry depends on a spiritually healthy pastor.

To start, you need to see your own spiritual health as much more than religious veneer for public display. Rather, you must value your own spiritual development as an essential ingredient for growing a satisfying life.

Once you begin to hunger and thirst for more of God, you can begin your search for someone who will hold you accountable in these areas. You don't have to settle for spiritual shallowness. Use the following raw materials to deepen and strengthen your faith.

Uncover Existing Spiritual Opportunities

You're exposed to faith-building opportunities every day in your ministry. Teaching and preaching take you to God's Word. This is the oxygen tank of spiritual health. You pray in public and in private; if you look for God's answers, you'll often see supernatural results. Counseling and pastoral care place you right in the middle of spiritual action, where you can see lives changed, marriages healed and spirits reformed. The challenge is to make better use of these close-at-hand opportunities to draw your soul closer to God.

Follow a Spiritual Fitness Regimen

Think of getting in shape spiritually in medical terms: A license to practice medicine, thorough knowledge of symptoms and illnesses, and 30 years of experience do not keep physicians well personally. They may practice medicine without being healthy themselves. For medical doctors to be healthy, they must apply to themselves the same rules that they give their patients, or they'll be as sick as their patients are.

The same is true of you. Your own spiritual growth is absolutely essential if you want to enjoy a satisfying and beneficial ministry. Simply put, to be spiritually fit yourself, you must seriously apply to yourself the remedies and suggestions you prescribe for others.

Retain Freshness

Your spiritual fitness requires fresh encounters with God in the faith-formation exercises of prayer, Scripture reading, worship, fasting and devotional reading. When you neglect these disciplines, you shortchange both yourself and your congregation.

Freshness may be more important than frequency. You must fuel your devotional practices with creativity, imagination, spontaneity, delight and even fascination. This means that spiritual wellness will take more than praying louder or longer. It will also require more than reading an additional 50 Bible verses a day.

Cultivate a God-Permeated Life

One pastor we know calls a close connection with Christ a "God-permeated life." What a word picture. This aspect of spiritual formation means getting together often with God. To use more informal language, you just hang out with Him. This God-closeness, like falling in love, creates attentiveness, togetherness and warmth. Your deepening intimacy with God will open your eyes to see amazing trophies of grace and will provide fulfillment throughout a lifetime of ministry.

This closeness to Christ results in more than a private adventure. It also allows divine enablement to flow through you into your ministry.

The Source for Lifelong Spiritual Growth—Christ

Your effort to keep spiritually fit activates Christ's extravagant promise, "Blessed are those who hunger and thirst for righteousness, for they will be filled" (Matt. 5:6). Just how can you know that sense of fulfillment?

Spiritual Health Illuminates Vision

When you're out of shape spiritually, ministry can seem blurry. What does God want from you and your church right now? Perhaps He wants something different. Maybe because of your dedication to get in shape spiritually, God intends to help your church clarify its mission. For example, your personal prayer efforts might ignite your ability to share the vision that God gives you.

What could provide more satisfaction than having God's guidance in carrying out His mission in your particular setting? How exhilarating to draw so close to God that you experience His blank-check promise that He will draw close to you!

Spiritual Health Leads to Well-Marked Trails

Spiritual growth generally makes use of established disciplines of the inner life. These disciplines take you along trails that saints have walked for generations.

Yet God also wants you to discover something incredibly new. Although many familiar landmarks lie along the paths of righteousness, new richness keeps showing up as you travel these well-known trails. God keeps infusing eternal truth with new light, brighter color and richer texture.

Spiritual Health Restores Balance

The confusing expectations and changing demands of being a pastor can easily get you off balance. Every reflective pastor is bothered by his use of time and by the feeling that ministry is never finished. And you thought only you felt that way!

So where does balance come from? It occurs when you start to see that *being* and *doing* are two interrelated dimensions of ministry. "Being" refers to who you're becoming in your personal relationship with Christ; it's a character issue. "Doing" refers to carrying out the many activities of ministry. Each informs the other, and both are vital in your ministry. The built-in creative tension between being and doing actually nurtures your growth spiritually.

Of course, spiritual fitness needs to be much more than some high-octane spiritual additive that you pour into the details of ministry. Instead, think of spiritual health as nothing more or less than living an authentic Christian life—normal, whole, well adjusted and Jesus focused—life as God intends it to be.

—⁓—

Conduct yourselves throughout the time of your sojourning here in fear; knowing that you were not redeemed with corruptible things.

1 PETER 1:17-18, *NKJV*

grace

understand
the hazards
of ministry

My extended family and lifelong friends live thousands
of miles away, and I haven't seen them for several years.
I thank God for the five pastors I meet with every other
week. They understand how tough ministry can be,
and we uphold each other in prayer.

PAUL, 46, WYOMING

Why is your spiritual health so important? Think about it. You may be wrestling with a crammed calendar, a hectic home, shattered dreams, starved intimacy and shriveled purpose. Regrettably, those may just be today's struggles. Who knows what tomorrow will bring?

Change at the Speed of Light

Think about what the world has been through in the past decade or so: terrorist attacks, sniper murders, school shootings. While these are national and world events, the instant and incessant replays on multiple 24-hour cable news channels means that these scenes affect you personally as well.

- *The world is different.* Not too long ago, few people had heard about the Internet. Who could have imagined that sexual temptations would be delivered to our computer screens? And who would have believed that such a high percentage of pastors would regularly visit steamy websites? Who would have guessed that a sex scandal would take place at the White House—and that the lurid details would be part of the news for months?
- *The church is different.* The church has seen its share of changes, too. Mainline churches continue to lose members. The divorce rate among church members isn't much different from the divorce rate of nonbelievers. And reliable research shows that the numbers of

Christians involved in premarital sex, cohabitation and emotional adultery aren't much different from those who never attend church.

- *Pastors face different realities.* Pastors of small congregations feel that they are being swallowed up by megachurches. Some shepherds want to change their biblical job title to that of chief executive officer. Worship wars, canned sermons printed off the Internet, the refusal to provide pastoral care, and the willingness to attract a crowd at any cost are among the strange viruses sweeping churches today.

- *People seem disinterested.* People certainly seem harder to reach these days. Their preferences and priorities shift quickly and profoundly. Surveys show that fewer people believe that there are unchanging moral absolutes, and more believe that moral truth is relative to circumstances. Two surveys conducted by Christian researcher George Barna revealed that "substantial numbers of Christians believe that activities such as abortion, gay sex, sexual fantasies, cohabitation, drunkenness

and viewing pornography are morally accept-
able." Based upon his research, Barna con-
cluded, "Without some firm and compelling
basis for suggesting that such acts are inappropriate, people are left with philosophies
such as 'if it feels good, do it,' 'everyone else is
doing it' or 'as long as it doesn't hurt anyone
else, it's permissible.'"[1]

These troubles can all seem so big that they make
us want to sing a mournful oratorio entitled "Ain't It
Awful."

The Hazards of Ministry

What's going on out there in the world and, sadly,
within many churches can make even the best pastors
want to fill ministry with activity that may be worthwhile but that ultimately accomplishes little for the
Kingdom. It would be easy to become a religious bell-
hop—serving the faithful few at church, while missing
the soul-stretching adventure of becoming a spiritual
leader for your community and beyond. As years roll
on, it would be easier to attempt to build a great
church rather than to develop robust, Christ-centered

people who will build a great church.

So, to gain an understanding of what's going on in the midst of these changes and spiritual war zones, you need to be aware of the hazards of ministry. Only then can you protect yourself from falling into these traps.

- *Walk-on-the-water syndrome.* This syndrome causes the people of a church to expect too much from a human being who happens to be a pastor. At the same time, the accolades can also lead pastors to believe that they're superstars. Walk-on-the-water syndrome triggers in some pastors a pseudoholy, prideful opinion of themselves. They allow themselves to believe the nice things that the people in their churches say about them. They think they're always right. They resist accountability.

- *Disastrous personal problems.* Secret sins, emotional brokenness and stress cause casualties among pastors. And the stress is multiplied as problems grow. An unsatisfactory reaction or terrifying circumstance in one area has a significant impact on other aspects of a pastor's life and ministry. A big fight with his spouse on Saturday night shows up in Sunday morning's preaching.

· *Distracted people.* Two-paycheck families face overstuffed calendars and long commutes. Many people are so overextended that they have no time to add another meeting or take on another phase of Christian service. When people are bombarded by commitments, going to church can become just another event on the calendar. Getting people to attend church more than once a week is an uphill struggle. Sometimes it's a battle to get them to attend even once a week, as the weekend becomes their family time. All of these distractions also undermine active involvement and stewardship.

· *Consumer mentality.* Consumer mentality saturates life today, and it's a reality for churches, too. When "consumers" come to church, they naturally expect programs and ministries to appeal to their widely varied interests. Few people choose a church for its biblical teaching or theological soundness. They may even feel uncomfortable with the biblical language of "sin" and "salvation." Instead, they choose a church on the basis of what it does for them, rather than what they can do for it. As a result, they also dodge serving. They don't want to teach Sunday School, work with the youth group or "babysit" in the nursery. They simply want a church that provides inspiration and encouragement for them.

- *Dysfunctional people.* The church attracts dysfunctional people because—at least ideally—it represents acceptance, love and belonging. But when dysfunctional people come to Christ, they bring their problems with them, and they look to the church for hope and healing. When churches ignore these pains from people's pasts, the unresolved issues pop up in strange and unexpected ways. Fallout from dysfunctional homes accelerates when pastors bring their own unresolved emotional baggage to their ministries. The result is that many churches have dysfunctional pastors leading congregations of dysfunctional people. Consequently, the personal and family crises pastors face every day with people in their churches terrify them. Some wonder whether ministry actually harms their own children, shortchanges their own marriages, or damages their own wholeness. Others desperately try to deal with their long-buried emotional difficulties. To make matters worse, many pastors don't seek professional help because they don't know whom they can trust with their inward secrets.

- *Sexual temptation and infidelity.* Our society seems to be drenched with explicit sexual information. Television brings visually stimulating smut into our family rooms. Internet pornography is as near as the computer in the den at home or in the study at church. Each week seems to bring heartbreaking news about another moral failure among pastors. In fact, infidelity by pastors may be the result of an accumulation of small marital problems that no one takes time to fix. Sadly, one morally bankrupt pastor ruins the credibility of a thousand and makes their work immeasurably more difficult. And those who are closest to the fallen minister (in the family or the local church) usually carry scars forever.

- *Unempowered ministry.* Physicians and lawyers can do their work based on education, practice and the good will of their patients or clients. But pastors need more. To minister effectively, pastors need vital and up-to-date contact with Jesus Christ. Unfortunately, pastors who travel around the religious block a few too many times can try to live without the power of the living Spirit. And nothing can be more frustrating than trying to lead a church without the power of the Head of the Church.

- *Leadership crisis.* Nearly every pastor is tempted to use power inappropriately sometimes. A self-centered craving to be in control—a problem that pastors find extremely frustrating in laypeople—can be even more poisonous to pastors. Remember that the apostle Paul's description of a leader is "fellow servant" (Col. 1:7). It's not "executive pastor" or "chief executive officer." Perhaps it's time to change the climate in churches where pastors seek prominence and power.

- *Loneliness.* Many pastors experience incredible loneliness. Occupational loneliness comes from serving a group of people who do not understand the demands of ministry. Geographical loneliness comes from serving miles away from extended family. Pastoral loneliness comes from serving people in crises. Like a chronic virus, loneliness troubles many pastors. One pastor said, "Loneliness feels like God is gone and has taken everyone who mattered with Him."

· *Superficial piety.* Being gifted, competent and reasonably nice are enough to make it in most professions, but intimacy with Jesus is the first requirement for ministry. When a pastor focuses on himself, becomes obsessed with personal needs or engages in self-aggrandizing talk about sacrifice or humility, he draws a congregation's attention away from Christ. Sometimes this kind of attitude comes from a deeply buried sense of weakness and inadequacy; the pastor feels the need to be the center of attention and to receive truckloads of affirmation.

Face Down the Hazards

You've read about the hazards. The challenge is to rise above them. Give yourself in service to Christ so that He can rescue people from the enslavements of sin.

Help those to whom you minister become established in a Christ-quality life. Immerse yourself in greatness. Keep remembering that love outlasts everything else.

Confront the hazards with God-provided courage, creativity, imagination and faith.

What needs to be done can be done.

Remember, the Lord called you. He honors you with a partnership with Him. You're a unique and extraordinary trophy of grace that God gave to your congregation. But that's not what makes you special. Rather, God's power at work in you is greater than any weapon in the world's arsenal. Don't forget it!

—⁓—

Each one should test his own actions. Then he can take pride in himself, without comparing himself to somebody else, for each one should carry his own load.

GALATIANS 6:4-5

grace

find an accountability partner

I've been blessed by God with a loyal friend for more than 20 years. He always believed in me more than I believed in myself. Eventually I became the person (and the pastor) he always thought I was.

ALAN, 62, OREGON

Whew! The undertaking of exploring the hazards that pastors face on the past few pages was exhausting. As you pondered the list, perhaps you recognized that you have been slipping into some of the traps that those hazards represent. Faced with those struggles—whether through circumstances you didn't choose or poor choices of your own—it would be easy to think, *Maybe it's just time to get out of the ministry.*

Again, however, your challenge is to rise above that. One wonderfully mysterious way that God helps you avoid the hazards—or heal after falling into them—is by giving you an unquenchable desire for relationships. Like everyone else, you need friends. Well-nourished relationships can add to your wholeness, keeping you emotionally whole and spiritually well.

We like the words we've read on an unsigned plaque:

A friend is one who knows you as you are, understands where you've been, accepts what you've become, and still gently invites you to grow.

Every pastor needs a friend like that—an accountability partner who will be an absolutely trustworthy friend. This is a friend you can voluntarily make yourself spiritually accountable to. Someone you can be totally honest with. The incalculable benefits of such a friendship include intangible payoffs like affection, trust, respect, mutual aid, understanding, devotion, acceptance, spontaneity and self-disclosure—all are components of wholeness.

Where can you find such a friend to hold you accountable to your Lord, your church and yourself? This person may be a mentor, a colleague, a neighboring pastor, a retired pastor, a childhood or college friend, or a peer in another denomination. Certainly, this soul friend is someone who loves you enough to be both tender and tough. He sees and responds when you need someone to pray with you or for you.

Because your soul friend has the goal of making you more authentic with his questions and warnings, you might find him by listening for someone who candidly says to you, "Be real," "Stop playing games," "Tell me what's really going on."

Seek out spiritually stable, well-adjusted people as sources of inner development. One of these friends might become your soul friend. Look for a spiritual strengthener who will stimulate your faith and bring accountability into your life. Look for someone who will be fair and honest in his evaluation of you and who will hold you accountable for your spiritual growth.

Ideally, your accountability partner will be willing to listen redemptively to your hurts, affirm your strengths and demand your authenticity. This friend must know when to pat you on the back and when to kick you in the seat. This person should be your best friend and your most demanding challenger.

Eventually, this friend will go to the mat for you, and you'll do the same for him. You'll willingly share pain and heartache as well as joy. You'll walk together through rough spots in parenting and problems in marriage. You'll grieve together and rejoice together, too.

In your accountability relationship, you'll enjoy a confidential, supporting, warming and bonding relationship that shows that you can count on each other unconditionally. A soul friend sustains you, supports you and makes you accountable—ultimately to the Lord.

—⁂—

We who are strong ought to bear with the failings of the weak. . . . Each of us should please his neighbor for his good, to build him up.

ROMANS 15:1-2

grace

empower your accountability partner

When an attractive young woman in my congregation began to flirt with me, I made myself accountable to my wife and to a fellow pastor. My ministry colleague calls me at unexpected times each week and asks me the hard questions—and demands my honest answers.

CLARK, 53, NORTH CAROLINA

While the concept of a soul friend sounds great, the truth is that building such a relationship may lead you over some pretty bumpy roads. In the midst of a busy ministry and home life, and faced with dozens of other demands, you now must nourish this unbelievably deep relationship. Is it really worth the effort?

The answer is a resounding yes. Establishing an accountability relationship provides a one-of-a-kind place for developing and using your spirituality. This relationship will help you become an authentic person, build inner integrity, strengthen your faith and help you see your relationship with God better.

As a special gift from God, this friend will be there to sustain you in dark hours, to help you cross-examine your thoughts and to lend support when you're afraid to believe in yourself or God. Simply put, this fulfilling relationship will provide fertile soil for growing a robust faith.

Make Your Relationship Work

To truly be held accountable by your soul friend, you must give him permission to ask about your relationship with God and to inquire about your holiness in living. In many accountability relationships, your partner gives you the same permission so that you hold each other accountable. Ideally, you and your soul friend will frequently question each other about your motives, your marriage and your ministry. Further, you'll ask one another about your use of time, as well as about times and places that you were tempted to cut corners, to rationalize your behavior or to dismiss your attitude.

More specifically, invite your accountability partner to start by checking where you are in the following areas of your life and faith.

Do You Really Know Christ?

Before you can develop spiritually in any other way, you must face the truth about whether you've ever truly accepted God's offer of a new beginning. Jesus said, "You must be born again" (John 3:7). The apostle Peter proclaimed, "In his great mercy he has given us new birth into a living hope through the resurrection of Jesus Christ" (1 Pet. 1:3).

This new beginning is a life-changing encounter with Jesus Christ—a spiritual heart transplant that changes your character so radically that new values shape your thoughts and actions. It transforms your existence at its deepest level. Far from diminishing life, knowing and accepting the gift of Christ lead you to an unimaginably deeper relationship with God.

Do You Really Believe That God Will Use You?

This question is important, because it counters the destructive self-talk that most people engage in. As you internally analyze situations, question experiences and debate alternatives, what deceptive self-dialogue creeps in to reinforce old and entrenched attitudes or lies? This doubting talk can start benignly enough; perhaps since childhood, you've told yourself that you're too tall, too short, too young, too stupid, too smart or too something. Later, the self-talk resurfaces in more cancerous ways: "I ruined my life by marrying the wrong person," "I'm a bad parent because my children are rebellious" or "I may as well not try in my ministry anymore, because I always fail."

As your accountability partner gets to know you better, he can challenge what you're telling yourself internally. Your friend can direct you to practice constructive self-talk, guiding you to tell yourself truths such as these: "I'm God's creation, and He doesn't make junk," "I'm making valuable contributions to my family," "I'm needed by someone" or "I always do my best; sometimes that's not good enough, but everyone makes mistakes." This kind of self-talk will lead you to confession, forgiveness and strength for a new start.

Do You Delight in Your Ministry?

Sadly, many pastors perform the tasks of life and ministry out of some ill-conceived sense of duty. As they carry out the responsibilities of their ministries—and sometimes even their marriages—all they can hear are the buzzwords "ought" and "should." This fixation on duty can create a stifling feeling that ultimately causes a second-class kind of living.

Your accountability partner can help you cultivate a perspective that turns duty into delight. For example, while your marriage is a vow and an obligation, it's also a God-ordained privilege that nourishes your inborn hunger for closeness and human intimacy. Although your children impose demanding long-term responsibilities, few things are more satisfying than forging life-long bonds with your children. And what makes the difference between drudgery and delight taking place in your ministry is your infusing meaning into it. That unexpected inner force that the apostle Paul promised becomes a reality as you do your work with joy: "I can do all things through Christ who strengthens me" (Phil. 4:13, *NKJV*).

Give Permission to Ask Searching Questions

An additional practical way your soul friend can hold you accountable is by agreeing on a set of questions that you'll ask each other each time you meet together.

For example, you might personalize the "rules" that John Wesley used in the early days of Methodism. While Wesley used his rules to establish converts in a group atmosphere of active faith and personal accountability, a similar process works well for an accountability pair as well. Wesley asked five questions in the class meetings:

- What known sins have you committed since our last meeting?
- What temptations have you met with?
- How were you delivered?
- What have you thought, said, or done of which you doubt whether it be sin or not?
- Have you nothing you desire to keep secret?

A more contemporary-sounding set of guidelines comes from Charles Swindoll. He used these questions with his staff and for himself, and he often shares them in pastoral conferences:

- Have you been with a woman anywhere this past week that might be seen as compromising?
- Have any of your financial dealings lacked integrity?

- Have you exposed yourself to any sexually explicit material?
- Have you spent adequate time in Bible study and prayer?
- Have you given priority time to your family?
- Have you fulfilled the mandates of your calling?
- Have you just lied to me?[1]

Or you might prefer the Ten Commandment-patterned guidelines developed by Rick Warren of Saddleback Church in California:

1. Thou shalt not visit the opposite sex alone at their home.
2. Thou shalt not counsel the opposite sex alone in your office.
3. Thou shalt not counsel the opposite sex more than once without that person's spouse being present.
4. Thou shalt not go to lunch or be alone in public with a member of the opposite sex.
5. Thou shalt not kiss anyone of the opposite sex or show affection that could be questioned.

6. Thou shalt not discuss detailed sexual problems with members of the opposite sex in counseling.

7. Thou shalt not discuss thy marriage problems with members of the opposite sex.

8. Thou shalt be careful in answering cards and letters from members of the opposite sex.

9. Thou shalt make thy secretary and thy wife thy protective allies in counseling.

10. Thou shalt pray for the integrity of staff members and colleagues in ministry.[2]

Finally, be sure that you clarify a very specific objective in your accountability relationship. Ask each other, "What's the desired outcome—the goal—for your spiritual development?" Remember, the idea of your relationship is to cultivate fertile soil for a growing and robust faith—the most basic ingredient of a fruitful ministry and a spiritually adventuresome life.

—⟋⟋⟍—

Submit to one another out of reverence for Christ.

EPHESIANS 5:21

grace

right
relationships

Our ministries can only be effective when our actions and reactions toward members of our families, our colleagues in ministry and the members of our congregations are pure. We must be clergy of peace.

Be of one mind, live in peace.
And the God of love and peace will be with you.

2 CORINTHIANS 13:11

Father God,
Help me keep focused on those You have given me in my home,
church, community and world. Enable me to love people—
imperfect, frail, holy, strange, faithful and sometimes devious.
Keep reminding me that I'm on a march to eternity with those
You have given me to serve.
Amen

unexpected
benefits

Life and ministry have been pretty good the past year. For three years now, I've pastored a small church in what some people call the Rust Belt. It's an older church in an established community.

In this church, I've had my share of faith-stretching times. While small churches are great because everyone knows each other well, they can also be places where everyone knows each other's business, too. That fact became one of the biggest blessings of my life.

Just over a year ago, my wife, Sharon, and I had our first child. It's unbelievable how that has seemed to bring out a lot of good in the people of the church. They've doted on our daughter, Emily, as if they were our extended family. It's like having several dozen grandmas, grandpas, aunts and uncles. Their love reaches out to us, as Emily's parents, in new ways as well.

Before Emily was born, Sharon had been working full time as a secretary in an elementary school near our home to help make ends meet. We'd come up with a financial plan that would allow her to cut back to half time as a teacher's aide when Emily was born. But for the last two months of her pregnancy, Sharon had to be on bed rest, which meant that all our financial plans went out the window.

Suddenly, the people of our church rallied around us in ways they never had before. They delivered meals, dropped off groceries and even anonymously left envelopes of cash at our door. Some of the women worked out a schedule to come in and clean our house.

The past year or so has made me realize something: No matter how long I'm here at this church, it is just as much a part of God's Church as any other local body. And I really love these people. I didn't always feel that way, but when Emily was born, I realized that I needed to start loving them as they love us.

On a typical Sunday morning about three months ago, when I was wrapping up my message from 1 Thessalonians 5, I read verse 11: "Encourage one another and build each other up, just as in fact you are doing." As I looked out over the 75 or so people, I stopped speaking. I realized that the people of this church had lived out that verse for my family and me, and a wave of unexpected emotions welled up from my heart.

I could tell that people wondered whether something was wrong. Finally, I was able to speak a bit and said, "I just want you to know that I love being your pastor. Being a part of this church family and having you care for Sharon, Emily and me is . . . well, I don't have words that can express how much I appreciate it. Having a part in helping you grow spiritually is the greatest joy I know. I thank God for bringing us here." That wasn't how I planned to close my sermon that day, but that was the ending.

My parents and grandparents were pastors before I became one. And I always wondered whether their talk about people loving their pastors—especially in the hard times—was really true. But now I know what the love of a church can be—the greatest benefit any pastor's family can have.

grace

why love
your church?

I thank God for reminders that I need to continue ministering with love and compassion to the people He has placed under my charge and care. I want to fulfill what Paul wrote to Timothy, "Watch your life and doctrine closely. Persevere in them, because if you do, you will save both yourself and your hearers."

TERRY, 47, CALIFORNIA

One of the things we like to say is that people are the main business of the church. Christ established the church for people. The work of the church is people. If people aren't helped, the church isn't doing its work. The church's ministry isn't just to keep the building in repair or the doors open. It's to win people. As a pastor, you've been given the privilege of befriending people, loving them, caring for them, winning them and building them up in the faith.

When a pastor and congregation don't love each other, the church suffers. Sadly, many pastors keep the people in their churches at arm's length. The result is that the people feel distant from their leader and the pastor feels isolated in his own church.

God wants your church to be a holy family, and He trusts you to be the spiritual head of that family. That means that, just like a parent, you need to learn to love the members of your family—warts and all. When you affirm and love the people in your church (and they affirm and love you in return), you'll both attract people to your church and love what you do.

People come to your church for a variety of reasons—location, the recommendation of a friend, or your church's programs of ministry. But acceptance and warmth are the reasons they keep coming back. And they're probably a big part of the reason that you stay. This means that you're a part of a unique community—your church—in which wonderful things can happen.

Stop and think for a minute about what your church is. Ideally, it's at least three things: a family of friends, a community of becomers and a society of love.

A Family of Friends

The church you lead and are a part of is a family of friends with at least two essential tasks: introducing people to divine resources and sensitizing them to human need. In many ways, the church helps people grow in faith, and at the same time, it offers to remedy the hollow emptiness of spiritually needy people. By stimulating authentic relationships, the church becomes a place where people come to understand that everything they possess are gifts from God. It's a place where He uses you "to prepare God's people for works of service, so that the body of Christ may be built up" (Eph. 4:12). In this extended family, fellow believers are closer than blood brothers and sisters. It's a place where people feel cherished and are offered a health-giving antidote for loneliness, isolation and tension.

This Christ-centered family offers the instruction of an exciting school where learning is a joy, the healing of a hospital where inner-health is assured, the resources of a bank where human needs are abundantly supplied and the acceptance of a home where love is supreme. As a network of friends, the church becomes a place where people strengthen each other in uniquely satisfying ways.

A Community of Becomers

Your church also has the potential to be a restoring community of becomers. This means that your church can be a place where you and others struggle together to be godly. As you examine your beliefs, aspirations, motives, emotions and choices, the relationships in your church provide a place where people can test questionable practices and create a climate in which everyone feels valued as a child of God. This unique blending of divine and human resources can't be found anywhere else.

Unfortunately, it's easy for churches to lose focus. The stirring adventures of life together become numbed by secondary concerns like traditions, bigger facilities and expanded programs. But an almost irresistible attraction emanates from authentic churches that are committed to caring for people rather than maintaining an institution. Your church's vigor and health—and your own as well—will only increase as the church gives itself to these lofty purposes.

A Society of Love

Your church can be a place where every relationship is infused with the love of Christ. Giving and receiving love in such an environment creates a supportive circle of healthy relationships. The church becomes a place where people affirm each other, encourage each other and show their love to each other in practical ways. As you meet together in such a fellowship of faith, you enjoy the privilege of saying warm words and doing helpful deeds that encourage one another to a deeper appreciation of the gospel, to stronger commitment of service and to lasting friendships centered in your common love for Christ.

——

So from now on we regard no one from a worldly point of view. . . . If anyone is in Christ, he is a new creation; the old has gone, the new has come!

2 CORINTHIANS 5:16-17

grace

here come the
joy suckers

*I pastor a rural church with 50 or less people in atten-
dance each Sunday. We battle continuity and consistency,
and it's often frustrating. Yet, after three years, we still
love it here. Sometimes I just need to hear those words of
encouragement, "Bloom where you're planted." I know
there's more blooming that God wants me to do here.*

WILLIAM, 28, MISSOURI

While we just looked at the many positive things that
your church can be, the reality is that it's not always
that way. People may be the main business of the
church, but there are some people who almost effort-
lessly create an atmosphere of negativity within it.
When left unchecked, this negativity can spread like a

fast-growing and aggressive disease.

Every pastor deals with people who create this kind of negativity. We jokingly call these people "joy suckers." However, nothing about them is very funny.

What's a joy sucker? Remember the movie *Ghostbusters*? The main characters who tried to rid unwanted ghosts from people's homes and businesses carried odd-looking machines on their backs. These contraptions had hoses and special rays that essentially sucked the spirits into their traps until the spirits could be contained elsewhere.

Joy suckers seem to have imaginary packs on their backs. They attach the hose to your heart, and in just a few seconds, all your joy is gone. It's amazing how much damage they can do to your heart and attitude in a short period of time.

Take a minute and close your eyes. This might be a little scary, but chances are you can picture every joy sucker you've ever pastored.

Hey, there's Mr. Jones. He's a joy sucker—always has been and probably always will be. You're headed to the front of your church just as the service is about to begin. Mr. Jones approaches you and says, "Pastor, I was walking up the sidewalk this morning on the way in from the parking lot, and I noted there's grass growing between the cracks in the sidewalk. So I was wondering, what do you plan to do about that?" Chances are, you just shake your head and move on through the service and the rest of your day. But deep down inside, you know that "grass in the cracks" is just a prelude to more negativity from that man.

After the service, another joy sucker, Mrs. Smith, walks up. You just had a great service. God was present, and you sensed that many people in your church were moved a step closer to the Lord. But here comes Mrs. Smith, worship folder in hand. Before you can even say, "Good morning," Mrs. Smith says, "Pastor, in the service this morning, I noticed that we sang several more of those praise choruses than hymns. I'd like to know what this church is coming to." Of course, you do everything you can to maintain your composure. Inside, you realize that this Sunday morning has been nothing but positive, yet one person missed a genuine blessing because she was so focused on herself that she couldn't receive God's beautiful gift to her. And you know that she'll spread her negativity to others in the church.

Is there a cure for a joy sucker? The truth is, joy suckers are unhappy people. Maybe they feel lost in life. Or maybe they were rejected by someone they loved.

Maybe they were disappointed by a previous pastor, a boss or a coach. Or maybe they just resent it when other people feel happy. For the most part, they have chosen to be just like they appear—suckers of joy.

You can see them coming. You try to hide, because you know that when your encounter with them ends, you'll feel negative and depleted. You don't want the joy sucker to turn you into a person you don't like. And regrettably, joy suckers have staying power—they seem to outlast everyone else.

If you're dealing with people like this, you may feel miserable about life—especially about your ministry. If you're still able to think straight about them at all, you realize that God could use most of these joy suckers in such positive ways if they would just decide to be different—if they'd just allow God to change their hearts.

What we all need to remember is that God didn't call us to live in negativity. He didn't intend for our ministries to be defined by naysayers. The writer to the Hebrews instructed, "Obey your leaders and submit to their authority. They keep watch over you as men who must give an account. Obey them so that their work will be a *joy,* not a burden, for that would be of no advantage to you" (Heb. 13:17, emphasis added).

It seems pretty clear that God doesn't desire that the church or the leaders of the church have the joy sucked out of them. If that happens, your church will simply look like the joy suckers. No matter how low these people have made you feel, you certainly don't want your church to resemble them. So how do you deal with joy suckers?

- *Love them because God does.* Ouch. You know that won't be easy, since the sight of joy suckers makes you want to run and hide. But think about it. When you love joy suckers, you can give them the benefit of the doubt, and you can do everything in your power to help them get well.
- *Try to understand where they're coming from.* Why does Mr. Jones act the way he does? Why does Mrs. Smith say the things she says to you? If you dig enough, you'll find that these joy suckers and others like them have something in their past that is reflected in their present.
- *Be honest with them.* Another tough one. However, you can't be afraid of the joy suckers in your church. Rather than avoiding them, you need to pursue them. You must work to

get them to change, rather than enabling a continuing pattern of dysfunction.

- *Set limits.* Ask yourself, *Am I going to allow the negative actions and attitudes of joy suckers to permeate this whole church? Or is there a limit?* While this decision could get ugly, you have to count the cost of what the joy suckers are doing to the rest of your congregation.

- *Surrender joy suckers to the Lord.* You can't heal or change anyone. You can only present alternatives and counsel. In the end, what joy suckers decide to do is up to them. You can only trust God to deal with them. However, as a caretaker of God's church, you can't tolerate or allow the poison of a joy sucker to infiltrate and destroy the fabric of the church.

Your job is to point men and women to a more positive and productive life in Christ. Of course, that's easy to say, but not so easy to do. Fortunately, you're just a custodian of the church God has given you to lead. The church is His. The people belong to Him as well.

So lift your head up. Define your ministry by the positive, not the negative. Almost every church will have at least one joy sucker. Just make sure the joy suckers in your church don't make a joy sucker out of you.

—⚬—

Give, and it will be given to you. A good measure,
pressed down, shaken together and running over, will be
poured into your lap. For with the measure you use,
it will be measured to you.

LUKE 6:38

grace

you really can love your church

I've just been through a few rough weeks of ministry, dealing with some tough situations in my church. Yet I'm humbled and thankful for the people of my congregation who love me and who faithfully stand strong in their faith no matter what trials come our way.

STAN, 41, TENNESSEE

We've explored some of the reasons why it's important to have healthy relationships in our churches. And we've admitted that some people can make it seem impossible to pursue healthy relationships—including people who are so negative that they seem to drain us of all the joy that should be found in ministry.

The reality is that some people are easier to love than others, and some churches are easier to love than others as well. By the way, the same is true of pastors. But because so much of a church's effectiveness depends on healthy relationships between you and your congregation, it's vital that you develop a love connection between your church and yourself. While this love relationship isn't the only thing that matters in your church, nothing else matters without it.

So, let's get practical. What are some ways that you and your congregation can love each other more?

Start Right—Could This Be Love?

When the first flicker of a call to a church comes to you, it's time to ask questions of yourself like these: *Could this be the start of something wonderful? Is God bringing us together? Will I fit here? Is this love at first sight? Is the chemistry right?* The answers will be uniquely personal.

Ask any married couple how they met and fell in love. The story will likely be unique—sometimes almost ludicrous. Even those who've been married 50 years may giggle like teenagers as they tell their story.

Interestingly, as the story unfolds, the relational ingredients of their relationship may not sound like a solid basis for a strong marriage. Yet that's exactly what they've built. How it looks to an outsider is not really that important.

In a similar way, strong, affectionate, spiritual-emotional chemistry between you and your church is needed at the start of the relationship. As in marriage, that ingredient will be unique; but you need to be convinced that a loving relationship can be established and maintained, or there's no point in going to a new assignment.

Say "I Love You"

Tell your congregation how privileged you are to be their pastor. We heard about one pastor who was always in love with his previous church and talked about it often. One person in his present church said, "Maybe he'll love us more after he's gone." The unspoken implication seemed to be "Maybe it should be soon."

A better approach is to speak up about your love for your present church. Then watch how much good comes. Every loving word reminds someone of the love of Jesus. Every loving word serves as a boomerang so someone in the congregation returns that love to the pastor. And every loving word grows the soul of the one who originates it.

Practice the words at home and in your study so that you can say without a hint of hesitation, "I love you with the love of the Lord."

Thank Your Church for Loving You

Do you live in a state of perpetual funk because you think that your church doesn't do as much for you as the church across town does for its pastor? Just remember, this attitude can be as silly as comparing two engagement rings. Sometimes it's the least costly one that represents the greatest level of devotion and love.

Or maybe you believe that your church should treat you like royalty—that you've paid your dues and the church owes you something for your years of service. Sorry, but that false notion doesn't sound much like the sacrifice, obedience and death to self that start at the Cross.

Instead, think of how rich you really are—a child of the King in service to the King's people. You preach from His pulpit and work in His office. You represent the King every day among His people. You speak for

Him and oversee His church. But you're wise if you always remember that you're not the King.

Be Worthy of Honor

Every pastor knows about the biblical admonition that the people of God are to give special honor to their spiritual leaders. Paul gave this charge in two of his epistles. In 1 Thessalonians he wrote, "We ask you, brothers, to respect those who work hard among you, who are over you in the Lord and who admonish you. Hold them in the highest regard in love because of their work" (5:12-13).

Again Paul suggested honor—even double honor— in 1 Timothy 5:17: "The elders who direct the affairs of the church well are worthy of double honor, especially those whose work is preaching and teaching."

We recall hearing the story of one lay leader who helped the church where he served do everything possible to honor their new pastor. But then he asked the church consultant who had helped the church find the new pastor, "Does anyone ever remind pastors that the Bible passages about honor have two sides?"

That faithful layman is right—the passage says that the pastor's side of giving honor is to work hard, lead the church and admonish the people of God. And double honor is for those who teach and preach.

In the day-by-day details of your ministry, the awe of being set apart by the sovereign Lord can grow dim. But you need to discover a renewed sense of responsibility for doing ministry so well that it pleases God. That will lead to a deepening realization of a final accountability for your pastoral service that can shape your long-term thinking.

Commit to a Lifelong Courtship

We were struck by the story of a couple approaching their sixty-seventh wedding anniversary. The husband, well into his eighties, was asked, "What advice do you have for younger husbands?" He replied, "You have to keep doing what you did to win her heart in the first place." There is much that is good and useful in that advice for your love relationship with your church, too.

But what about times when feelings of love have evaporated? The advice of a syndicated advice columnist to a woman who had fallen out of love with her husband applies to pastors, too. The counsel: Stay where you are. Start acting as if you're in love. Do loving deeds. Show love until warm feelings start growing again. They will.

Preach Love

Go back to the Bible. Feed your soul as you check the love passages. Teach your people over and over that love for one another grows naturally out of God's love. Show them that love is a gift to be received from God and to be passed on to the people around you. Try building a spiritual atmosphere in your church that fulfills the challenge of Ephesians 5:2: "Live a life of love, just as Christ loved us and gave himself up for us as a fragrant offering and sacrifice to God."

Become a Whole Person

Character counts, and character is the wellspring of conduct. Chances are that if your congregation had to choose between a skillful pastor and a holy pastor, they'd choose holy.

In this age of unprecedented dysfunction and brokenness, the church sometimes becomes the last stop for hurting, confused, messed-up people. And what a welcome refuge it is for them. As a result, many of these people find a brand-new life in Christ and start living a life of new beginnings. But in the process, some have a persistent problem or two—a habit, a scar, a tender spot or a secret sin. If you're in that group, do whatever it takes to find mending in those broken places and healing for those hurts.

On your way to wholeness, you also need to be utterly dependent on God. If you try to do ministry in human strength, you'll never be able to give enough. Remember that as a pastor, it's that something extra in your life—the grace, presence and power of God—that will make you victorious and effective and will help convince people that what you preach is authentic and true.

Paul put it this way: "Set an example for the believers in speech, in life, in love, in faith and in purity. . . . Devote yourself to the public reading of Scripture, to preaching and to teaching" (1 Tim. 4:12-13).

Do Your Congregation a Favor— Try to Understand Yourself

How do you think? What are your predictable reactions? What's the driving force in your life? What are your motives?

Self-understanding is an important key to understanding others. Question your motives by asking yourself, *Why did I do that?* Cross-examine yourself about the way you lead meetings. Check yourself on how you spend your money—it reveals a lot about your character. Ask yourself whether you manipulate administrative tasks to get your own way and then justify your action by calling it the will of God.

Remember who you were when you were called? Remember how God used your love for Him to help you see the needs of His world? What a defining moment for your ministry! That day, God summoned you to unknown territory with the promise to be with you, to empower you and to love you no matter what.

Recalling His amazing love and care can help you keep your ministry focused. When the love dimension seems to be burning low, do a reality check and get your love glowing again. Here's that reality check: God loves you. Most (if not all) of the people in your church love you. And you get to love them back.

Wrap your arms around your ministry. Love the people whom God has given you to serve, and they will love you back in ways that go beyond your loftiest dreams.

—⁂—

Encourage one another daily, as long as it is called Today, so that none of you may be hardened by sin's deceitfulness.

HEBREWS 3:13

grace

love your family
even more

*Out of the blue this morning, my wife called
my office and said, "Thank you for loving me and our
family." I'm not sure what prompted her to do this,
but it definitely made my week!*

GENE, 34, ILLINOIS

We're going to say something you already know: A pastor's work isn't easy. Financial stress, lack of privacy, feelings of isolation and a sense of inadequacy are common among pastors. These stressors often extend to their families as well. A report from the Pastoral Care Division of Focus on the Family reported that in recent years, the most prominent calls to their toll-free phone line dealt with issues of marriage, child-parent relationships and commitment to the pastoral call. A nonscientific survey of pastors' wives on Focus's website for pastors, *The Parsonage*, revealed their concerns about the lack of time they spent with their spouse and the effect that exposure to church conflict might have on their children. Family members can feel neglected and pushed aside by the work of the church. In addition, if the pastor's spiritual life is empty and the problems at work are brought home, families suffer. Not only is ministry difficult, but it also can be hazardous to the health of pastors and their families.

If you see yourself in these words, what can you do? In reality, a healthy family exists only on a pastor's wish list until it is a lived-out relationship, characterized by love and hard work among those who occupy the same household. What's needed most is a commitment between you and your spouse to live out your love for each other and your children. This is essential, because whatever your family has—either good or bad—is contagious in your church.

Of course, like most things in life and ministry, loving your family more than your church is easier to say than it is to do. But consider these practical steps that can help you:

- *Speak up.* Speak up in your marriage relationship so that it's clear what each of you needs and wants. Talk to your kids, too. Help them know that your love for each other is the strong glue that holds everything together in your family. And tell the people of your church that you can serve them better when relationships are going well at home. Let them know that you want to build and maintain a strong marriage and family, for yourself and for the sake of your ministry to them. Reasonable people will honor and appreciate that priority.

- *Strive for contentment in your marriage.* Both your ministry and your marriage will flourish when you feel unconditional love from your spouse. Being married to a contented person is more fun than constantly dragging a partner out of the swamp of frustration and despair.

- *Keep the gender war outside your relationship.* The so-called battle between the sexes in society has allowed cynical attitudes and caustic talk into too many pastor's homes. Keep these hostile attitudes out of your relationship. Make it your most important issue to build your own great marriage.

- Seek solutions and satisfaction. If you want to take a giant step forward, you must gulp, take a big breath and look objectively at your marriage to identify difficulties and possibilities.

  God gave you marriage for companionship, pleasure, procreation and long-term joy—be sure not to miss the delight and satisfaction that He intended for you to experience. Perhaps it would help to write out the innumerable blessings that ministry offers to a marriage.

- *Tear down competition between marriage and ministry.* Refuse to allow ministry and marriage to be in competition. Since God made the gospel so people-focused, the relationships in the pastor's home are a microcosm of the family of God. Your home is a place where family members can demonstrate, enjoy and even test love. Every bit of time, money or effort you invest in your family is an investment in the health of your church. Most, if not all, of your people want their pastor and spouse to model Christian marriage.

- *Set an example of a great marriage and family.*
  Remember, people in the world and members
  of your church will be drawn to authentic
  faith, inner attractiveness, fulfilled marriages
  and solid families. Since that is true, why not
  consider building an ideal marriage as part of
  your commitment to be an example to the
  church you serve?

- *Count your blessings.* We just mentioned the
  idea of making a list of blessings that ministry provides to your marriage and family.
  Flexible time, unique opportunities to influence people's lives, an extended family to love
  you at church, special church guests who visit
  the pastor's home and the opportunity to
  share in shaping the church's future ministry
  are some that come to our minds. Cherish
  these privileges and the other blessings that
  your unique situation provides. Talk about
  these advantages often in your home with
  your spouse and children.

- *Make time to develop your marriage.* Some pastors and spouses find that it helps to create a
  weekly time-island of spiritual, emotional
  and physical intimacy where they spend time

alone together to catch up on all dimensions of their marriage.

- *View your family through your church's eyes.* Look at your relationship with your spouse and your children through your church's eyes. Ask leaders in your church to talk to you about family, and put their suggestions to work. View your family as a living segment of society that is headed by you.

—∞—

*Houses and wealth are inherited from parents,
but a prudent wife is from the LORD.*

PROVERBS 19:14

grace

a servant-shepherd's heart

The example that the Good Shepherd gave to His followers was, in the first place, that of a servant—the towel, the basin and a sincere willingness to be humble (John 14)—and in the second place, that of an overseer who carefully watches his flock.

I lay down my life for the sheep.

JOHN 10:15

Lord,
Give me a shepherd's heart like Jesus'. I want to serve as
He served and lead as He led. The people I lead sometimes
need the rod of correction and at other times the staff of guid-
ance. Help me know the difference. Deliver me from a
CEO mentality. I'm grateful to serve as an undershepherd
of the Shepherd. Thanks be to God.
Amen

tending
the flock

About a year ago I was looking for a new church.

After a good three years in ministry at this church—my third in a series of stepping-stones—it seemed that all I was doing was focusing on little details. We'd grown a bit—enough that we'd hired a part-time worship leader, and we were searching for a full-time youth pastor.

In fact, it was the youth pastor situation that got me thinking about leaving. I was looking for prospective candidates, and I found myself dreaming about how much greener the grass might be if I were to head to the proverbial other side of the fence.

I think one of my strongest gifts is being a visionary. The problem is, when you're the one dreaming big dreams, you start to see yourself as top dog. When I wanted something done, I became convinced that I was right—so right that I demanded that things be done my way.

A year ago I ran into some obstacles. I really wanted to hire an associate pastor to help me with what I thought were the draining details of church life. But one strong-willed parent in the church convinced our board that we needed a youth pastor instead. "Convinced" is a good word for it—that mom pretty much talked the congregation into hiring a youth pastor.

When I started looking at classified ads and asking around our denominational network about good youth pastors who might be looking for a new challenge, I started seeing ads for senior-pastor positions. On paper, the churches looked bigger and better—and certainly the people would appreciate my gifts and dreams more than my current congregation seemed to.

But a funny thing happened. As we invited a couple of candidates to visit our church, I started to see things from a new perspective. In fact, one Sunday as I drove up to the church building, it was almost as if I hadn't been there before. As I said good morning to the usual early birds, I realized that these were live, flesh-and-blood people—God's people! I met with the youth-pastor candidate in my study, and I couldn't keep from bragging about the people of my church. I even boasted about the parent who almost single-handedly convinced the congregation that we needed a youth pastor!

That day I realized that during those years of ministry, I'd largely lost the sense of what it means to be a shepherd. I'd forgotten what it means to care for a flock. And maybe most important, I'd forgotten that God had entrusted this flock to my care.

After the services that day, I lingered in my study just to spend a few minutes alone with God. I found myself praying something that struck me so powerfully that I've made sure to request the same from God many times since. "God, show me what You want done as I care for Your flock today."

Since then, the routine of serving here feels new each day. Before, I thought I was being a good pastor by making my vision happen. Now I know that being a pastor means so much more. As I tend this flock, I feel that our opportunities are huge and that the results will be eternal. Why was I ever satisfied to settle for less than that?

grace

called to be a
servant,
called to be a
shepherd

When I was called to be a pastor, I felt like a marked man. The trouble is that no one else could see the mark but God and I. Yet so far I've enjoyed more than 20 years of working out the meaning of that wonderful encounter with God.

ROBERT, 50, PENNSYLVANIA

Who are you? You're probably well trained, competent and professionally credentialed. It's likely that you drive a late-model car, wear nice clothes and have an impressive education. Many people view you as the professional that you are, similar to a doctor, lawyer, social worker or teacher. While this sounds splendid, the danger is that you can become more committed to being a person of respect in your community than being an all-out disciple of the Lord.

We recall reading that some pastors are so concerned about career development that when they are approached about going to a new place of ministry, the first thing that comes to their minds is the four Ps: pay, parsonage, prominence of pulpit and pension benefits.

While these issues are legitimate concerns, they can't become the determining factors. Your calling as a pastor means you must start with questions of obedience and service and the guidance of the Lord. That's the lifelong satisfaction of living out your calling.

So what is your calling?

Called to Be a Servant

Jesus provided the best illustration of what it means to be a servant when He said,

> I have set you an example that you should do
> as I have done for you. I tell you the truth, no

servant is greater than his master, nor is a messenger greater than the one who sent him. Now that you know these things, you will be blessed if you do them (John 13:15-17).

Humility and servanthood go together. In fact, it's hard to know whether service produces humility or if humility motivates service. The two belong together, and it seems impossible to have one without the other.

There's no more profound example of leading with humility and being a servant than the story of Jesus washing His disciples' feet. We call those who follow Jesus' example the Towel Company. It started in the heart of Jesus in the Upper Room when He washed His disciples' feet. To become a Towel Company member requires no stock purchases, initiation ceremony or well-connected recommendations. It simply starts by doing something for someone else in the name of Jesus.

By taking this simple kind of action, you reject the widely accepted notion that one individual can't affect society. One person *can* affect society—including you! In fact, one social scientist recently expressed the opinion that the quality of a whole culture can be changed if just two percent of the population has a new vision of what needs to be done and starts doing it.

Servanthood, as it shouts from the pages of Scripture, is God's crowning pattern for finding fulfillment. The disciples thought that place, power, prominence and authority brought satisfaction. But Jesus taught them an entirely different way of finding true greatness and fulfillment, when He said, "The greatest among you will be your servant" (Matt. 23:11). Don't miss the three-dimensional fulfillment: a helpful deed you do for a fellow human being, a gift you give to God, and a satisfying favor you do for yourself.

Ministry can be especially exhilarating when a great cause consumes you. This idea is captured by the English statesman James Bright: "You should link yourself to a great cause; you may never do the cause very much good, but the cause will do you a great deal of good."[1]

When James and John requested honored places of authority, Jesus used haunting words to explain a Kingdom principle: "Whoever wants to become great among you must be your servant, and whoever wants to be first must be your slave—just as the Son of Man did not come to be served, but to serve, and to give his life as a ransom for many" (Matt. 20:26-28).

Leading and serving are permanently tied together. At all levels of church life, genuine leaders are servants. Our Lord tied true greatness to the royal road of service. Therefore, the real Christian leader has a desire to serve—an attitude that both the Church and the world find attractive.

Called to Be a Shepherd

Jesus also provided a pattern for what it means to be a shepherd. In John 10, Jesus spoke of the shepherd and his flock. You'll recall that the word "pastor" comes from this analogy of shepherd and sheep; it is the Latin word for "herdsman."[2]

Let's look at three qualities of a shepherd. First, a shepherd keeps constant watch over his sheep. In biblical times, a shepherd was never off duty; he lived with his sheep. Even today, a good shepherd always meets the needs of his sheep before he meets his own needs or wants.

Second, a shepherd practices patient love. He knows his sheep, and the sheep know the shepherd. The shepherd does whatever he can to gain the trust of his sheep. Jesus explained, "The sheep listen to his voice. He calls his own sheep by name and leads them out. . . . His sheep follow him because they know his voice" (John 10:3-4).

Third, a shepherd displays selfless courage. He guards his sheep against threats, such as wild animals and thieves. "The good shepherd lays down his life for the sheep" (John 10:11).

In Jesus' well-known conversation with Peter, Jesus also used the analogy of caring for sheep (see John 21). He asked Peter three times, "Do you love me?" Three times Peter replied, "You know I love you." Each time the Lord gave a clear directive that ultimately shaped Peter's ministry: "Feed my lambs," "Take care of my sheep," and "Feed my sheep" (vv. 15-17).

Later, after many years of growing his soul and maturing his ministry, Peter testified to pastors of all generations, including ours: "Be shepherds of God's flock that is under your care, serving as overseers—not because you must, but because you are willing, as God wants you to be; not greedy for money, but eager to serve" (1 Pet. 5:2).

Your love for God is measured by how well the sheep under your care are tended and fed.

Living Out Your Calling

Maybe you've heard John Frye's simple statement, "Pastoring means taking God to the people."[3] This means moving from the world of studying and preaching to the world of helping stressed and weary people to experience Immanuel, God with us. Consider these simple and practical strategies for taking God to your people.

Search Your Heart to See If God Can Trust You with More People

We know a pastor with a mission-minded congregation. His church has helped resurrect a dying church in a neighboring town by giving people, prayer and affection. In addition, the church gave money and sent work teams to refurbish the other church's building. When we asked what it was like during those first few weeks when the core people for the new church were gone, he replied, "The Lord has helped us replace the people we gave."

Think about this other profound insight that the pastor gave: "I believe God will give a church as many people as He can trust them to care for." If he's right, the effectiveness of your evangelism is at least partially determined by the quality of the pastoral care you provide.

Contact As Many People As Possible at Church

In small- to middle-sized churches, contacting as many people as possible means contacting everyone. Greet people before the service, after the service and during fellowship times. In conversation, don't be afraid to add a pastoral touch such as "How are you doing spiritually?" "I prayed for you this week" or "I'm counting on you to pray for me while I preach this morning." Make eye contact, and touch people by shaking hands, placing your hand on their shoulders or giving appropriate hugs.

Use the Phone Creatively

Make it a point to call 10 people every day; you can accomplish this in about 30 minutes. If you reach a message machine, express your care with a comment such as "The Lord brought you to my mind this morning, and I just wanted to tell you that I prayed for you today."

If you know that some people are working, call them at their places of employment. Initiate the call with a greeting such as "I was thinking about you this morning. Do you have a minute for me to pray briefly with you right now?"

Write a Note

Hand-addressed first-class mail always gets read. A handwritten note positively affects the receiver way out of proportion to the effort that writing it requires. Try to write at least 10 brief notes on Sunday afternoon to thank people for ministry that morning. Don't be surprised if some people keep those notes for years. Or if speed is a concern, you can write dozens of "personal" notes in a short time by copying and pasting the same text into the body of an e-mail, and personalizing it by changing just a few words.

Contact Everyone Regularly

With a bit of organized effort, your church can contact every member every month. You can accomplish this even if you pastor a larger church. One church in California grew rapidly to more than 500 active members because they used a phone bank system at the church. Everyone—members as well as prospects—received a call every Saturday.

Use the Ripple Effect

Contact visitors and other prospects directly, but disarm them by saying, "I'm in the ministry to help as many people as possible. Do you know anyone who needs a pastor to help them or pray with them?" When they tell you about someone who needs help, be prepared to follow up on that lead. Often, before the conversation ends, they'll admit that they have a personal need. Be sure to give them your business card so that they can call you when they think of others who need you.

You'll be amazed at how taking God to the people will renew and fulfill your servant-shepherd's heart.

—∞—

Be shepherds of God's flock that is under your care, serving as overseers—not because you must, but because you are willing, as God wants you to be; not greedy for money, but eager to serve; not lording it over those entrusted to you, but being examples to the flock.

1 PETER 5:2-3

grace

uniquely gifted
for ministry

*Every so often I get caught up in the trap of comparing
my ministry to bigger churches in town—and even
across the country. But then I realize that God has given
me a wonderful flock to undershepherd for Him, and I
have the greatest calling in the world.*

KEVIN, 39, TEXAS

God is amazingly creative. Even though He created a
blueprint for how pastors should relate to their congregations as servants and shepherds, He didn't create
cookie-cutter pastors. In fact, He loves variety.

God made you different from every other human
being. God created you to be a unique person so that
He could use you in a special way. He doesn't want you

to imitate someone else. Instead, He wants you to yield to His will and purpose so that He can help you accomplish important things for His kingdom.

We recall a TV commercial that showed four children who were asked what they want to be when they grow up. One responded, "I want to be a fireman." Another, "I want to be a doctor." The third, "I want to be a basketball star."

Then the fourth answered, "I want to be myself."

Think about the insight behind that last answer. As a pastor, you must cherish your uniqueness and not try to copy anyone else. But how do you do that in a practical way? Here are some ideas for you to consider.

Cultivate Your Uniqueness

When God created you, He put together a plan for a distinctive ministry for you. He wants you to do something special for Him—something that no one else could do as well as you. It might surprise you to hear that He likely wants you to accomplish your ministry right where you're serving Him now. No one else is capable or gifted to accomplish what God has mapped out for you.

God believes in your gifts so much that He chooses a risky strategy for changing His world through you.

He allows you immense freedom to discover how you'll use the gifts He has given you. He places unique desires in your heart, and then He grants them. The psalmist said it well: "Delight yourself in the LORD and he will give you the desires of your heart" (Ps. 37:4).

If you don't tap into these God-given gifts, you'll feel bored and unfulfilled. When you fail to use your unique giftedness, both the Kingdom and your congregation suffer. The results are that your ministry is less effective and you deny your congregation the gifts that God intended for you to use in your ministry.

Excellence Brings Satisfaction

God wants you to give your best in every part of your ministry. When you do less than your best, it reflects poorly on God and His kingdom—not to mention your congregation and yourself.

Why not give God your excellence as well as your faithfulness? He multiplies satisfaction for those who do their work well. Giving less than your best is a habit, but giving God your excellence can be a habit too. Doing your ministry well will produce incredible impact for the cause of Christ, even as it brings you indescribable exhilaration.

Realize That You're Not Perfect

Have you ever played the perfection game? It's a game that can paralyze you with self-imposed demands, causing you to feel that you must act as if you know everything or pretend to be more pious than you really are. When faced with a situation that you have no experience or training to deal with, you bluff your way through to make a good impression. Sadly, the game usually will beat you, eroding your self-confidence and draining your satisfaction.

Of course, the reality is that no one can do ministry perfectly all of the time. When you admit your weaknesses to your congregation, you may be surprised to find that they'll simply overlook your inadequacies with a shrug. In fact, they'll be relieved to hear that you're human, too. Pretending to be perfect will just wear you out. When you're tired and worn out, you're unable to accurately evaluate your work and ideas. So without intending to do so, you create a fantasy of who you are, what your church can be and how important you are to your church.

There's a fine line to walk as you serve. Your intention should be to do the best work in ministry that you're capable of doing at that moment. You serve people who are in need, and you serve in Jesus' name. Both the people and the Lord deserve and need your best. Of course, you understand that your best will never be good enough without the Spirit's help. Yet you can also never be satisfied to do shoddy service simply because you can't do it perfectly.

Challenge yourself to come to terms with your lack of experience, your weaknesses and your toxic need to be perfect. Take it to the Lord. Remember, He has given you every gift, talent, ability and experience for you to thrive in the ministry to which He has called you.

Keep Stretching in Ministry

In addition to understanding that God has uniquely gifted you to serve right where you are, realize that you haven't arrived yet. Even the apostle Paul admitted that he had much more to learn when he wrote,

> Not that I have already obtained all this, or have already been made perfect, but I press on to take hold of that for which Christ Jesus took hold of me. Brothers, I do not consider myself yet to have taken hold of it. But one thing I do: Forgetting what is behind and straining toward

what is ahead, I press on toward the goal to win the prize for which God has called me heavenward in Christ Jesus (Phil. 3:12-14).

To maximize the personal spiritual potential of your ministry, preach every sermon to yourself before you preach it to others. Teach every lesson knowing that the study of these ideas will make you more like Christ. Offer pastoral care with the assumption that you'll learn a lot about God by seeing Him at work in the experiences of needy people. Lead the administrative work of your church with a dependence on God's guidance. See ministry as a living encounter with Christ in the human and spiritual dilemmas of church life. Grow your own soul as you work with the holy mysteries of grace that you offer to others.

Appreciating your unique gifts and taking the opportunities that God gives you to grow spiritually will result in professional growth and amazing insight into yourself. As you reflect before the Lord on who He has uniquely—even "fearfully and wonderfully" (Ps. 139:14)—created you to be, what you learn will help you continue to grow professionally, emotionally and spiritually. And you'll thrive in your service to Him and to your congregation.

—⟋⟍—

In your teaching show integrity, seriousness and
soundness of speech that cannot be condemned, so
that those who oppose you may be ashamed.

TITUS 2:7-8

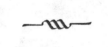

grace

you're a leader, so lead!

For the first time in years, I spent a day alone a couple of weeks ago for sort of a personal spiritual retreat. I read the whole book of Acts, and it struck me that God worked through very ordinary people and made them leaders of the Church. I asked Him to cleanse me of times I try to make things happen without His leading and to provide the Holy Spirit's power instead. I'm already beginning to see a change in my ministry!

JOHN, 44, MICHIGAN

God calls you to ministry—to be a shepherd and servant to your congregation. And He uniquely gifts you to fulfill that ministry. At the same time, He calls you to be a leader—something else you don't ever want to forget.

Your church needs you to be a leader. It needs you to be much more than a resident saint who shows up for church, maintains the establishment and spends the money. Instead, your church needs an authentic leader who, at every level of life and ministry, establishes and communicates vision.

Not all leadership starts with being given an important position, although some of it does. A person can hold a pastoral position for a lifetime without ever being a leader. Consider the following ways to become a genuine pastor-leader in your church.

Be a Christ-Saturated Leader

Being a Christ-saturated leader is a wonderful gift that you can give yourself, your family and your congregation. A Christ-focused pastor will find ministry to be more productive, more gratifying and more magnetic. Think of what the Holy Spirit's abundance will do in your ministry. He invades and enriches every thought you think, every decision you make, every emotion you feel, every action you take, every opportunity you experience and every reaction you have.

To evaluate your life and ministry as a Christ-saturated leader, honestly ask yourself the following questions:

- Does personal prayer energize my preaching and pastoral service?
- Do I practice periodic fasting of food, desires and activities in order to focus more on Christ?
- Am I more like Christ than I was six months ago?
- Do I cherish my own spiritual mentors, and do I work as a spiritual mentor to others?
- Do I check Scripture to see if my practice of ministry in leading, preaching and teaching is biblical?
- Am I as committed to my own spiritual development as I am to my professional development?
- Do I measure my ministry by the stories behind the numbers?

See the Church and World as Living Classrooms

To increase your competency when it comes to leadership, keep alert to life. Listen carefully for leadership lessons from people of all walks of life. Apply insights from every source to your ministry. Be aware of and adapt from pastors who are trendsetters. Observe and implement the best ideas of pacesetters in business and government.

As an achievement-driven leader, you'll take what you learn from life and apply it to ministry. As an imaginative pastor-leader, you'll gladly consider any concept, program or principle that can improve your ministry. As you continually ask yourself how you can make your ministry better, you will help formulate your church's future.

Be a Passionate Risk Taker

A reluctance to take risks, a fear of pioneer frontiers and a refusal to retool ministry shackles the work of God. The Church needs more leaders with a do-or-die, breakout spirit.

What can keep you from attempting great things for God? When fear strikes, ask yourself these questions: *What's the worst that can happen? What's the probability that the worst thing will happen? What can I do to keep the worst from happening? What are the possibilities if I don't take risks? What's the potential for achievement when I'm willing to take a risk for the cause of Christ?*

To keep your leadership courageous, pray these six short, adventuresome prayers. They will shape you into

Christlikeness, demand your best efforts, revolutionize your life and direct you to creative ways of doing ministry.

1. Search me.
2. Break me.
3. Stretch me.
4. Lead me.
5. Use me.
6. Take me to the frontlines.

Beyond your managing, influencing, directing, preaching, administering, and teaching, as a true leader you'll challenge people to embrace hope, love, belief, compassion, wonder, reverence and grace.

By reaching deep into these never-dry, ever-fresh springs, you can equip the people of your church to truly be fully devoted followers of Christ.

—⁓—

When the Chief Shepherd appears, you will receive
the crown of glory that will never fade away.
1 PETER 5:4

grace

partners in
ministry

*A couple of weeks ago, as I was driving past our
church facility to run an errand, God brought to mind
the people who make the church what it is. I'm
amazingly blessed to have so many people who willingly
step forward to serve with me in ministry.*

LYNN, 56, GEORGIA

To be a leader, you need time to lead. That means you'll
joyfully and willingly delegate many ministry tasks to
others in your church. Without question, your church
will be healthier spiritually when you share ministry
with church members. You'll empower the people in
your church and increase their spiritual development,
and more ministry will get done.

Yet you can't delegate all ministry to others. You can't bloom and grow when you only manage and assign ministry to others. You don't need to do all of the ministry—and you can't. But you must do some of it. When you no longer minister to others on a regular basis, you forfeit a key ingredient of ministry; you give up a spiritually satisfying bond between yourself and the people of your church that can't be replaced in any other way. To give up this essential connection means giving up something precious and needed for personal fulfillment.

However, your commitment to staying involved personally doesn't deny service opportunities to others. The paradox is to continue personal ministry while giving much of it away. You need to delegate, and your congregation needs to participate in the day-to-day life and ministry of the church.

It might sound scary to think about giving away so much of your church's ministry. But just imagine what your church would look like if every member was truly a minister. If you like that picture and you want to empower the people of your church to serve, here are three seeds that you can plant in their hearts:

1. *Everyone has a place.* God has prepared a place for everyone in your church. Encourage the

people of your church to wait before Him and ask what He wants for them and where He wants them to serve. Encourage them, as Jesus encouraged Peter, to let down their nets (see Luke 5:4). Challenge them to look for the miracle that God has in mind for each of them: "No eye has seen, no ear has heard, no mind has conceived what God has prepared for those who love him" (1 Cor. 2:9).

2. *Everyone has a gift.* Each person is uniquely qualified for the opportunities God gives them. Your job is to help the people of your church discover their gift or gifts. Urge them not to worry about how many or what kinds of gifts they have. Instead, challenge them to spend time doing what they do best so that they make the most of every God-given opportunity before them. Help them err on the side of doing something—it's better to run the risk of wearing out than rusting out.

3. *Everyone has a dream.* We recall a song by the Cooper Brothers that says, "The dream never dies, just the dreamer." When it comes to the people in your church, you don't

want to be the dream killer. Instead, encourage people to get in touch with God's dreams for them. Remind them that if God's dreams seem impossible at first, if they truly come from Him, He will make a way. The world may stomp on their dreams; it may even destroy some of them. But it can never take away the power that causes the dreams to occur in the first place. Remind them that the world will play with their dreams and even cause them to wonder if it pays to dream again. It does! Urge them to dream on.

When you intentionally release and empower people to do ministry, both you and the people of your congregation will discover something remarkable: Service offers its own satisfaction. It rewards the servant with personal growth and spiritual development. The satisfaction of service takes people beyond fulfilling a duty and performing tasks to doing something they love.

Real service does three important things that you need to demonstrate in your own life as well as teach your congregation: First, it pleases God. Second, it has an impact on others. Third, it sharpens the spirituality of the servant.

Satisfying service is an incredible fringe benefit of the Christian life. Serving gives the server satisfactions that can't be found anywhere else. Most of the people in your church will never discover this surprising fringe benefit until you highlight it for them or help them discover it in the gratitude of someone they serve in Jesus' name.

—∽∾—

As we have opportunity, let us do good to all people, especially to those who belong to the family of believers.
GALATIANS 6:10

PART 4

grace

constant
safeguards

We must be vigilant. To put on the whole armor of God is not merely an option; it is a necessity if we are going to successfully obey the command of our Lord to flee the various onslaughts of Satan.

Be strong in the Lord and in his mighty power.
Put on the full armor of God so that you can take
your stand against the devil's schemes.

EPHESIANS 6:10-11

Gracious Father,
Deliver me from the fascination of the forbidden, the seduction
of sin and the silly need to impress my peers. Give me an
untainted mind, a pure heart and a worthy reputation. By
grace, help me live a lofty life that's pleasing to You and inspir-
ing to those You've called me to serve.
Amen

avoiding
ruin

I'm looking for a new job, and it won't be in the ministry. I'm sending out resumes and waiting for phone calls.

Just a few months ago, I was secure in a new church, thinking I'd spend many years serving there. But everything started to fall apart when a counseling situation became a gripping relationship. As this situation began to get out of control, I knew that I had to do something drastic. Things would only get worse if I didn't stop it quickly and decisively. I realized that it could ultimately lead to the destruction of two families, a church and my ministry.

I'd actually thought about the possibility of a sexual relationship with the woman I was counseling. I was afraid—afraid of my own feelings, afraid to tell someone, afraid not to tell someone, and afraid of what would happen if I did tell.

When I considered all the angles and prayed beyond my emotions, I decided to call the area supervisor of my denomination and tell him that I was in trouble and to risk whatever the end result would be. I looked at the phone for about an hour, dialing all the numbers but the last and stopping. Suddenly I dialed all the numbers, and he answered on the first ring. "Al, this is Robert. This isn't a normal call. I'm in trouble."

As I told him my story, he advised me to tell my wife. Maybe we could keep things within the circle of the two couples and go on with what appeared to be a promising ministry. That night I told my wife, and the "other woman" told her husband. I'll never forget that night—all hell seemed to break loose. It was clear that this wasn't going to be contained between the two couples.

I shared with my board honestly and with a repentant heart. I did all I knew to do. They accepted my apology and believed I was right with God, but they felt that my ability to minister there was diminished. Some said that they still loved me but that they could never see me as their pastor again. My heart was broken. I loved these people.

As I look at all that has happened in recent months, I feel a total loss and lack of direction. I'm even angry, because I did face down the temptation without sinning. I don't think it's right to be cut off from all our Christian friends at this troubled time. At times, I question God and wonder why we must face such financial hardships and loss of self-esteem when I did what I felt was right.

I just hope that my story can help another pastor avoid ruin and realize how high the stakes really are. Maybe it will help someone realize that we must avoid even the appearance of evil. Before you do something you'll regret, consider the high price of any inappropriate action. You could lose your ministry on the basis of even a suggestion or accusation.

Establish safeguards before you need them. The decisions about how you'll counsel need to be made long before you get into the counseling relationship. In many cases, if you have to ask, "Is this going too far?" it has and it will be hard to turn back.

These days, I'm trusting two promises as I cling to my faith: "A broken and contrite heart, O God, you will not despise" (Ps. 51:17) and "The LORD upholds all those who fall and lifts up all who are bowed down. The eyes of all look to you, and you give them their food at the proper time" (Ps. 145:14-15).

grace

the need to flee

I went through some rebellious times a number of years ago. A lay leader in my church at the time was brave enough to ask me questions such as "Who are you accountable to?" "How is your relationship with God?" and "Is your strength coming from Him?" I'm pretty sure God used that man to save my ministry.

DANIEL, 62, MAINE

Chances are, you've heard about and maybe even known pastors who just give up because they can't or won't control destructive urges in their lives. But why would anyone jeopardize everything that matters for a few moments of pleasure—putting profession, ministry, family and reputation at risk?

The answer isn't simple, but it's fairly easy to explain. When these pastors come face-to-face with temptation in their lives—when in the back of their minds they hear "Run!"—they choose not to flee.

What does it mean to flee? It means turning around and running because something is after you. It could mean that you're in some kind of danger or that you're being pursued by something stronger than you are.

It's at these moments—when the devil seems perched on your soul, trying to convince you that wrong is right—that you need to listen to the familiar and dependable counsel of the Holy Spirit, who warns, "Run! Run as fast as you can! Move away! Don't stand there for even one more minute!"

Consider the following areas from which Scripture clearly says to flee.

Flee Immorality

First, look at 1 Corinthians 6:19: "Do you not know that your body is a temple of the Holy Spirit?" But did you know that Paul wrote this passage in relationship to sexual immorality and misconduct? Ephesians 5:3 is like an echo; it says "There must not be even a hint of sexual immorality."

These are vital words to remember and obey when Satan begins to whisper tempting things in your ear. His whispers are the beginning of a trap. What would you do if you unexpectedly found yourself in a compromising counseling situation with someone of the opposite sex? Or if you opened an e-mail only to find a link to a pornographic website? In these situations, would you be trapped? Or would you flee?

Flee Idols

Paul made another warning in 1 Corinthians 10:11-14:

These things happened to them as examples and were written down as warnings for us, on whom the fulfillment of the ages has come. So, if you think you are standing firm, be careful that you don't fall! No temptation has seized you except what is common to man. And God is faithful; he will not let you be tempted beyond what you can bear. But when you are tempted, he will also provide a way out so that you can stand up under it. Therefore, my dear friends, flee from idolatry.

This is a tough one for pastors, because when it comes to idolatry, we don't think we need to worry. We believe we're strong enough to withstand the assault on our faith. We think, *I don't need to flee from that. I'm strong enough. I've got what it takes to counter that temptation. I'll just adapt and take control.* But the truth is that we're no more resistant than anyone else.

Right now, you can probably think of three or four people you know well who moved away from lifestyles of faith into old lifestyles of rebellion. They fell prey to their former ways. Why? Because they didn't think the rules applied to them. They thought they were adequate enough to handle the temptations that they were facing, but they failed.

You can't handle it! That's why Paul said to flee idolatry. Don't stand there. Don't let it affect you. Flee it. Take the way of escape. "He will also provide a way out so that you can stand up under it" (1 Cor. 10:13).

Flee Materialism

Paul also warned about materialism:

> People who want to get rich fall into temptation and a trap and into many foolish and harmful

desires that plunge men into ruin and destruction. For the love of money is a root of all kinds of evil. Some people, eager for money, have wandered from the faith and pierced themselves with many griefs (1 Tim. 6:9-10).

What do having an unhealthy attitude toward money and desiring material things do? Idolatry over material things can cause you to make bad decisions about additional employment, debt, expenditures, investments and ministry. It can destroy you when you have little, and it can spiritually wreck you when you have plenty. An arrogance and pride about "things" can sneak into areas of your life and cause you to see yourself as better than others because of what you possess or control. Materialism can erode or even destroy you.

If this is an area that you don't flee, Satan will wave dollar signs and power signs in front of you with destructive consequences. Materialism can destroy your motivation, your priorities and the person God intended you to be.

Fleeing is not just about resisting sexual temptation. It's about turning from those things that pollute our minds and tarnish the Kingdom values that we invest in. In this case, the passion for things can relegate

God to a lower status, and ministry to a business rather than a call.

Again, Paul listed the way of escape: "Flee from all this, and pursue righteousness, godliness, faith, love, endurance and gentleness" (1 Tim. 6:11).

Flee Evil Desires

Finally, Paul warned us to flee evil desires. "Flee the evil desires of youth. . . . Don't have anything to do with foolish and stupid arguments, because you know they produce quarrels" (2 Tim. 2:22-23).

Paul wrote that the evils of bitterness, rage, anger, fault-finding and jealousy will dominate your heart and destroy the basic fiber of who you are (see Eph. 4:31; 5:5). You'll become something you're uncomfortable with—someone you don't even respect.

The way of escape is this: "Pursue righteousness, faith, love and peace, along with those who call on the Lord out of a pure heart" (2 Tim. 2:22).

The Answer

Scripture is filled with warnings, but as you've seen, it also comes with answers. James wrote, "Submit yourselves, then, to God. Resist the devil, and he will flee from you. Come near to God and he will come near to you" (Jas. 4:7).

When Satan knocks at the door—and he will—he'll use every trick in his seductive scheming to destroy what God envisions as holy and clean. When you don't slam the door and run, you give Satan a toehold; and in that moment of innocent acknowledgment, you can be hooked.

Run! Flee!

Remember Christ, who went to the Cross for you. Think of the sacrifice He paid for you and His unconditional love for you. He is the One who has trusted you with your ministry. He cries out to you to flee. Run as fast as you can away from the evil one. Flee into the safety of God's care, for that is where your safety lies.

When evil is pursuing you, look around. For there is also the loving presence of your heavenly Father, who promises,

> No temptation has seized you except what is common to man. And God is faithful; he will not let you be tempted beyond what you can

bear. But when you are tempted, he will also provide a way out so that you can stand up under it (1 Cor. 10:13).

—◈—

Be imitators of God, therefore, as dearly loved children and live a life of love, just as Christ loved us.

EPHESIANS 5:1

grace

credibility
and character

*The other day, as my 10-year-old headed off to school,
I was struck by the fact that he's more than halfway
toward becoming an adult. I realized that he deserves a
dad who models godly character for him—not just in the
public arenas where being a pastor leads me, but also
in the darkest and deepest corners of my heart.*

RICK, 43, ARIZONA

In theory, all pastors would like to measure up to the
standards that Paul set for Timothy in 1 Timothy 3:2-3:
"Now the overseer must be above reproach, the husband of but one wife, temperate, self-controlled,
respectable, hospitable, able to teach, not given to
drunkenness, not violent but gentle, not quarrelsome,

not a lover of money."

But in reality, of course, pastors are under siege. As we've already observed, many pastors battle with temptations that not only test their credibility but can also dilute or destroy their ministries.

While sexual sins of pastors often make big headlines, these aren't the only temptations in the ministry. Even built-in temptations make pastors easy prey for ethical downfalls. For example, stresses in your marriage can cause problems. Loneliness can also make you vulnerable. We commonly hear from pastors who say that they can't find a close friend. And the absence of accountability systems can contribute to the problems of temptation. Spiritual lone rangers need trusted friends to ride beside them.

Ironically, while you feel alone in the ministry, people in your congregation may place you on some sort of superhuman perch. This means that you're seen as a winner if your church enjoys spiritual vitality and growth. But you're a loser if you fail to exude constant enthusiasm and attract more members. And while you're supposed to feel energized by ministry, sometimes meeting the needs of other people saps you of inner resources and creates a spiritual drought. Maybe you've had times when you've felt betrayed by the very people you serve. Maybe you've had members of your church treat your family poorly or question your free time.

All of these situations can be trying. You might as well admit that you're not immune to the pressures that can lead to moments of weakness—split seconds when you might give in to a moral or ethical temptation.

Being aware of these situations suggests that you should work to build defenses in your day-to-day ministry to prevent moral lapses that can prevent you from enjoying God's best for you.

Rooted in Character

The apostle Paul set a good pace: "I do not run like a man running aimlessly; I do not fight like a man beating the air. No, I beat my body and make it my slave so that after I have preached to others, I myself will not be disqualified for the prize" (1 Cor. 9:26-27).

You and your church need you to follow Paul's outline, with the objective of aiming for spiritual and emotional health, effective service and a strong finish. The following tools can help you reach your goals.

Be Shaped by Scripture

As an authentic follower of Jesus, you see yourself as God's servant in a particular place. You view yourself as a bond servant to Jesus Christ, a shepherd of the flock and a steward who manages the affairs of your Master—all scriptural metaphors. In addition, you listen closely to what Scripture requires and promises. You desire to give attention to serving the Master well in every detail of your life and ministry, not just in your teaching and preaching.

Make Ministry a Way of Life

While ministry is both a profession and a calling, it's also complete immersion in a great cause. Even though you might try to get away from it, ministry is always with you. It stays on your mind and invades your free time. Like parenting, ministry never leaves you—it's there day in and day out, year in and year out. You can either happily accept this fact or accept it with kicking and screaming, but it's still a fact.

View Christian Service as a Gift from God

The ministry is a bit like a three-legged stool. First, it's something you do for God—you serve others because it pleases God. Second, you serve to meet a need in someone else's life. The third component is easy to miss: You serve because you're personally enriched in the process of serving others. So you preach for God; but when you preach, the Word seeks you out, and your soul grows in the process.

Check God's Perspective of Your Assignment

When God sends you somewhere to serve Him, He already knows all about that place. And He already knows all about your abilities, background and potential. When you take an assignment that seems to be in God's will, ask yourself and God what He had in mind for you to accomplish there. Then ask why you'd want to leave before you fulfilled His plan for you in that place.

Know Your Sources of Strength

Your sources of strength are prayer, Scripture, intimacy with God, a coach or mentor, and a satisfying marriage and family. All of these should help you be stronger and better and more useful for God. Build on the foundations of commitment, character, competence and content. There's a good chance that you, like every other pastor, have an inner personal need to strengthen one or more of these essential areas.

Live Above Reproach

Living above reproach never restricts your ministry. Instead, it frees your ministry. A life above reproach makes ministry easier, because it draws people to your authenticity. It doesn't squeeze the adventure out of ministry; it gives you a heart that stands without shame before God and with no regret before the people of your church.

Archibald Hart noted that every expression of pastoral integrity will toughen your spiritual awareness:

> A healthy concern for morality is not enough to maintain a ministry of integrity. Each pastor has a responsibility to develop a personal code of ethics tailored to his unique set of circumstances.
>
> Simply wrestling with such a personal code begins to sensitize one to important issues. Over time, there begins to develop an "ethical sense"—a natural ability to tell if any action is likely to become a problem.[1]

An authentic current relationship with God is the basis of pastoral power that will affect every phase of your ministry. It's the source for Christlike character, joyous Christian experience, lifelong commitment to your call to ministry, and robust faith.

Make holy character the bedrock foundation of your ministry. This character, made pure and empowered by God, will have a magnetic attraction to the people in your church, home and community.

—⁘—

Count it all joy when you fall into various trials, knowing that the testing of your faith produces patience.

JAMES 1:2-3, *NKJV*

grace

strategies for
guarding
your heart

*I want how I think and live to be so visible and so
shaped by God that if I'm ever accused of something
inappropriate, the people of my church could say,
"His high standards of behavior prevent him
from being capable of such conduct—he's
incapable of doing what you say."*

MIKE, 51, OHIO

Just as physical exercise is essential for the conditioning and endurance of a star athlete, so mental, emotional and spiritual exercise also are imperative for you
as a pastor. Conditioning yourself in these ways will

enable you to meet the demands that test your limits.

One overstressed pastor understood the pressures of ministry, as evidenced by his statement: "Ministry sometimes feels like being chased by an unfriendly Doberman."

Fortunately, God promises to come alongside you to strengthen you and empower your ministry. Trying to do ministry in your own strength won't accomplish much. But when you allow God to overcome the obstacles in your life, He will supernaturally strengthen you.

How can you practice any kind of spiritual conditioning in the midst of your crowded life and hyperbusy ministry? Let's start with some personal strategies for guarding your heart.

Live by a Code of Integrity

Developing a personal code of integrity starts when you commit yourself to self-imposed guidelines that provide you with a sense of moral control of your life. This code becomes ingrained in you. When tests and temptations come, as they will, you'll never need to reconsider, negotiate or fantasize about giving in. A code of integrity builds holy conduct into the fiber of your life before temptation appears.

You don't practice integrity to protect your public face, to reassure your spouse, to impress your children or to convince your church of your personal holiness. While a code of integrity may accomplish all of this, it's a personal commitment to yourself and to God that you will be what you say you are.

A good place to start to build your own code of integrity comes from asking yourself the same questions a friend or colleague might ask you in an accountability relationship (see pages 61-64).

Maintain Your Resistance

Remember James 4:7? It reads, "Submit yourselves, then, to God. Resist the devil, and he will flee from you." In the biblical context around these verses, James promised that God gives grace to the humble (see v. 6). Then James wrote that if you submit to God and draw near to Him, He will draw near to you (see vv. 7-8). Finally, James instructed that if you humble yourself before God, He will lift you up (see v. 10).

Keeping close company with the Father keeps up resistance. When you keep your spiritual resistance high, Satan can't overcome you (see 1 John 5:18).

Although the devil is strong, he's not invincible. As Jesus demonstrated in His temptation, the devil will get lost when confronted with God's Word and a no-intention-to-give-in kind of resistance from the person being tempted (see Matt. 4:1-11).

Maintaining spiritual health requires you to keep your exposure to the viruses and germs of sin to a minimum. Keep your distance from the sources of infection. Watch your company. Monitor what you view on TV according to God's values. Be careful about what you read and view on the Internet.

When temptation does come, go to God's Word to renew your resistance. Ask your accountability partner for help. And if you're married, ask your spouse to pray for you.

Control Your Appetite

Controlling your appetite means committing not to become a victim of your glands or a slave to seductions. It means allowing God's power to keep you from senseless sin and stupidity. What right-thinking pastor would choose infidelity rather than the life-time affection and intimate satisfaction found in marriage?

Make an airtight commitment to protect your marriage. This means being thoroughly Christian in your thought life, conduct and influence—including the emotional support of your family. Be vigilant to monitor your behavior and continually realign yourself to the purposes of God. Your goal is to have pure motives and holy character.

Strive to Maintain Balance

We believe there's a direct correlation between fatiguing burnout and moral failure among pastors. On a radio broadcast, after psychologist Dr. James Dobson outlined the countless roles performed by an average pastor, he warned, "The pastorate is built for burnout, it's built for exhaustion, and it's built for trouble."

He's right. Fatigue, burnout and frustration in ministry can make a pastor more vulnerable to falling prey to moral lapses. If you're feeling tired, working too many hours, feeling sorry for yourself, wondering if your work is worthwhile, or no longer praying, it's easy to let your guard down.

You must practice balance for yourself—no one else will force you to do it. Here are several useful ideas for balancing your time:

- *Office hours.* Keep regular office hours so that work routines and time at home are predictable. When conflicts arise, solve the crisis, and alter your schedule so that your spouse or children aren't cheated of your time and attention.
- *Family.* Schedule time with your family just like any other priority item in ministry. Establish a date night each week with your spouse, and schedule time weekly with each child. Years will pass at breakneck speed with your kids, and you can miss a lot before you know it.
- *Priorities.* Allow for shifting priorities in your schedule. Fixed priorities can create major conflicts. Try keeping one day a week open just to be able to shift demands. While you always want to keep God in first place, there will be times when you need to give a big chunk of time to marriage, family or a crisis in your church.

Balancing ministry is a lifelong quest. Ted Engstrom, longtime president of World Vision, noted, "For a leader to excel, he must find avocations and interests in his life away from the job. He must not only provide materially for his family, but give them much of himself as well."[1]

Although you'll seldom completely achieve balance, the simple act of striving for balance each day and each week will make your life more balanced than it would be with no plan.

—m—

Among you there must not be even a hint of sexual immorality, or of any kind of impurity, or of greed, because these are improper for God's holy people.

EPHESIANS 5:3

grace

how others can help you guard your heart

I'm a dad, a husband and a senior pastor—and I wear many other hats, too. Sometimes I feel like I'm on autopilot—especially when it comes to intimacy with my wife. We went to lunch last week, talked for a long time and decided to make conscious improvements in our relationship. For one, we're going on a date every week, no matter what!

JAKE, 37, MINNESOTA

In the previous chapter, we discussed some strategies that busy pastors can practice to stay in excellent spiritual condition. Let's continue with some strategies for guarding your heart that others can help you with.

Ask for Help

Of course, the first step in just about any problem situation is admitting that you need help. However, this step can't come only when you're in trouble. In fact, asking for help long before temptations arise will allow you to have established relationships with godly people who will be prepared to help you through the most trying times.

In addition, in many places these days, you can find good, biblically based help for sexual temptations, ailing relationships and any other problems you're facing. Build a resource list of parachurch ministries, Christian counseling services, trustworthy and well-trained fellow pastors, and denominational counseling services. This is a good exercise for finding help when a hurting member of your congregation needs it, and it can serve you if you ever find yourself over your head in temptation.

Cultivate an Accountability Partnership

We've already said how important it is to have an accountability partner. Remember, this is someone to whom you've given permission to ask about your relationship with God, your prayer life, your marriage and your commitments to your family. This relationship is a commitment between you and another person of the same gender to seek a special enabling of God's power on your respective ministries and families.

This kind of covenant relationship is based on mutual trust. You and your accountability partner should commit to pray for each other on a regular basis—at least daily. Meet at least once every two weeks for a time of sharing. Between meetings, keep in touch with encouraging phone calls, e-mails and notes in the mail.

This relationship can be simple. The key to the effectiveness of having an accountability relationship is that both of you are willing to say, "I believe in you enough that I will allow you to really know who I am in Christ."

Keep the Home Fires Burning

Although this subject is seldom discussed, without knowing it, pastors and their spouses often carry unresolved intimacy frustrations from their bedrooms into their ministry. One pastor's wife said, "I carry on a cold war of pettiness and small terrorist acts because my husband flirts with a woman in church and never meets my physical needs at home."

One pastor wrote,

> My wife and I both had brief emotional flings with people in the church. We could have avoided this so easily if we'd gotten help to work through our needs for affection and caring at home. She needs more affirmation and affection from me, and I need more sexual gratification from her.

We hope that these individuals represent a minority. Preventing these kinds of problems, however, requires an increased concern for the needs of each spouse. Sexual frequency and technique aren't nearly as important as mutual satisfaction and an eager willingness to please each other.

One way to enrich your marriage is drawing up a marriage covenant. Although no suggested list will work as well as one you and your spouse discuss and promise to each other, this sample list can be a good starting point for establishing and maintaining a healthy marriage:

- God will always be the honored guest in our home.
- We work as a team in ministry.
- We are committed to each other for life.
- We will never shut the door on communication.
- We will make time to meet each other's spiritual, emotional and sexual needs.
- We will encourage each other to develop our individual gifts.

The ways that you guard your heart—both personally and with the help of others—can help protect you, your family and your ministry by keeping you from doing something cheap, questionable or immoral.

These strategies can help you live beyond reproach. They will please God, authenticate your ministry in the minds of the people of your church, reassure your spouse and family, and generate great fulfillment in yourself.

—∿—

Flee the evil desires of youth, and pursue righteousness, faith, love and peace, along with those who call on the Lord out of a pure heart.

2 TIMOTHY 2:22

grace

embrace God
intimately

The deeper one's relationship with God through His Son Jesus, the more successful he will be in living a life above reproach and setting "an example for the believers in speech, in life, in love, in faith and in purity" (1 Tim. 4:12). An intimate relationship with Him makes it all possible.

Come near to God and he will come near to you.

JAMES 4:8

Holy Father and Head of the Church,
Give me a passion for Your presence. Help me live and serve so that I may have Your mind and do Your will. Ministry without You is boring and frustrating. Ministry with You is adventuresome and fulfilling. I choose the adventuresome and fulfilling.
Amen

delighting
in God

I was one of those pastors who always look ahead. I attended every seminar that my church or I could afford (and some we couldn't).

I daydreamed of becoming a Chuck Swindoll, Bill Hybels or Rick Warren. I spent hours at my computer, writing down ideas for books. I pored over maps and prayed that God would lead me to some great place to serve Him. I even rationalized that I wasn't totally carnal or egocentric, because I did study Scripture to try to figure out how the New Testament Church had grown.

One day in my personal study time, I was reading in the book of James. Suddenly, James 3:13-16 jumped off the page as if I'd never seen it before in my life:

Who is wise and understanding among you? Let him show it by his good life, by deeds done in the humility that comes from wisdom. But if you harbor bitter envy and selfish ambition in your hearts, do not boast about it or deny the truth. Such "wisdom" does not come down from heaven but is earthly, unspiritual, of the devil. For where you have envy and selfish ambition, there you find disorder and every evil practice.

Oh, man, did I feel the Holy Spirit tugging at my heart! These words seemed to be welded together on the page of my Bible, and they were red hot, branding my heart as I read them over and over: "selfish ambition," "earthly, unspiritual, of the devil"; "selfish ambition," "disorder and every evil practice."

The Spirit was working—I knew I had to keep studying—but I desperately wanted to get out of James. I thought I'd turn to a psalm for comfort. Imagine my surprise when I read this in Psalm 37:3-4:

Trust in the LORD and do good; dwell in the land and enjoy safe pasture. Delight yourself in the LORD and he will give you the desires of your heart.

I realized that all these years of looking ahead to when I would someday be a great pastor, I'd never really done what these verses say. I was looking everywhere except to God. I never really saw the church where I was serving Him as a place I wanted to dwell very long. And I certainly never enjoyed tending the flock that He'd given me. Don't get me wrong—they're great people. I just never really stopped looking ahead long enough to love them.

But the second verse in this passage really got to me as I connected it back to what I'd read in James 3. Certainly my earthly and unspiritual selfish ambition was not a desire that God wanted in my heart.

Well, my story has a pretty happy ending. I've been working hard at trusting and delighting in God, rather than in my selfish goals. I've put away the maps and accepted that where I'm serving Him now is where He wants me to be—at least for now. I've been trying to see the people of my church through God's eyes—and I must say that I do enjoy them and my ministry to them much more than I ever imagined.

Ironically, another passage in James sums up pretty well what I've been trying to do.

Submit to God. Resist the devil and he will flee from you. Draw near to God and He will draw near to you. Cleanse your hands, you sinners; and purify your hearts, you double-minded. Lament and mourn and weep! Let your laughter be turned to mourning and your joy to gloom. Humble yourselves in the sight of the Lord, and He will lift you up (4:7-10, *NKJV*).

I'm serious, all right, Mr. James. But strangely, by whispering yes to God, I'm more content than I've ever been. The games may be over, but the pure fun is just starting. And maybe for the first time in my ministry, I am on my feet—sometimes all day and well into the evening—and I love every minute of it!

grace

a hunger to embrace God

*A few years ago, God grabbed hold of me somehow
and placed in me a desire to really know Him better.
This sounds funny coming from a pastor, but I want
to have an authentic relationship with Him. I want
the meaning and fulfillment that come from
a deep relationship with Christ.*

JAMIE, 48, COLORADO

We live in a day when many people—even those who call themselves committed Christians—suffer from an inner sickness of the soul. Song publisher John Benson describes this plight as an "unsatisfied, mysterious me—an uncommitted, unfulfilled self at the core of human experience."[1]

As pastors, it's easy to be frustrated by this vague vacancy of the spirit. Filling this inward void requires more than we can think with our brains or feel with our senses. It requires an intentional embracing of God.

Turning toward God is the first step toward faith, potential and creativity in ministry. Finding fulfillment starts by embracing God—taking your unsatisfied, inner emptiness to God's abundant resources for growing a satisfying life and ministry. This can lead to much more meaning than you might imagine. It answers Paul's prayer for us "that the eyes of your heart may be enlightened in order that you may know the hope to which he has called you" (Eph. 1:18).

As you open every part of your life to God, you'll discover a unifying center for your thoughts, values and commitments. Embracing Him can strengthen you and give you a sense of wholeness no matter how difficult your life and ministry seem to be.

Rediscovering the Power and Renewing the Passion

Embracing God means pursuing and enjoying intimacy with Him. It means traveling on the most magnificent human pilgrimage imaginable—a Christ-saturated way of living. Much more than mere empty theory, embracing God results in seeing and experiencing life differently. It means allowing God to remake you into what He wants you to be and the person you want to be.

Consider how embracing God can strengthen your soul.

You'll Become a Spiritual Change Agent

What would happen if you again fell madly and passionately in love with Christ? What would the result be if you lovingly and willingly opened your life in complete obedience to Him? What if you asked the Lord of life what changes He wants you to make in yourself and your church? To be genuinely in love with the living Lord is to want to please Him. If you're willing to do that, He'll use you to win your world and renew your church.

You'll Focus Every Aspect of Your Life on Christ

When you fully embrace God and continually seek to be more like Christ, rather than experience an out-of-focus, watered-down and out-of-balance faith, your life and ministry will be strengthened and empowered. When you embrace Him with your whole heart, He'll enter the darkened, secret places of your life and help you realize that you have almost everything you need—except intimacy with Him.

Embracing God will also enable you to see Him at work in every strange, wonderful, puzzling, extraordinary or common circumstance of life and ministry. This means that even when you don't totally understand what God is doing in you, you accept that He never wastes a relationship or situation in developing your interior life.

You'll Develop a Healthy Dependence on Scripture

You accept God's Word as your reference point for living. As you faithfully study Scripture, God will make it part of your inner vocabulary and thought processes. You'll find yourself thinking God's thoughts and living them out in the details of your ministry. In surprising ways, scriptural truth will come to mind when you least expect it but when you need it most. Fully embracing God means looking to His Word for specific help today, but you benefit because its strength also accumulates across your lifetime. A passage learned as a child comes back to you like a sweet refrain of an old love song—because that's exactly what it is.

You'll Feel an "at Homeness" with God

All people need a sense of their roots so that they know where they belong. Like everyone traveling through the human experience, you have a pressing need to know where you started and where you're going. In some satisfying and mysterious way, embracing God can provide a starting place, a pilgrimage and a destination. But it also provides an "at homeness" along the journey. And while you can gladly acknowledge that one day you'll be at home with God, you can also have the sense that you're at home now—with the constant nearness of Jesus, a connectedness with the people of God and a sense that you're moving toward the final exam and the reunion that follows.

You'll Learn to Laugh at the Obstacles

What obstacles can you name that have always prevented you from fully becoming who Christ intends you to be? It might include poor parenting, a sibling who mistreated you, poverty, growing up in an undesirable neighborhood, a low IQ, or some social handicap that you think you can never change.

However, when you draw close to God, He might show you that your biggest obstacle is something you seldom admit but is just the thing He wants you to change. These might include fear, selfishness, pride, anger, self-pity, unconnected guilt, exaggerations and doublespeak.

The following ideas are ways that God can provide solutions for these obstacles.

- *Resist excuses.* Recognize and own the obstacles when God points them out to you.
- *Ask God for empowerment, and do what He tells you to do.* The process of making things right helps condition you not to do the wrong again.
- *Never give up the spiritual ground you've gained.* There is no need to drive five miles on a spiritual flat tire when you can repair it on the spot.
- *Take positive action.* Sincerely congratulate someone you envy. Correct an exaggeration or overstatement immediately. Confess and apologize for sins of the spirit.
- *Don't let obstacles control you.* Own the obstacles in your life, talk about them, expose them, refuse to give in to them. The more you refuse to give in to them, the less power they have over you.
- *Replace a negative thought with a positive one.* Replacing a negative thought with a positive

one sounds too simple, but it often works. Place the focus of your thoughts and actions in the direction in which you want to move.

- *Offer your obstacles to God for cleansing and healing.* It's a giant step of spiritual progress when you're willing to admit that you don't want to hang on to attitudes, emotions and fears that harm your intimacy with God. Give up your enjoyment of pride, self-centeredness and envy so that you can become what God has in mind for you to be.

You'll Experience Renewed Energy in Ministry

It's easy for ministry to be predictable, duty driven and even apathetic. God deserves something more—like creativity, imagination and effectiveness. As a response to intimacy with God, commit to doing something significant for Him. True service is a love gift to God—one He doesn't need, but one you should be delighted to give.

Embracing God will open your eyes and affections to new adventures and opportunities of serving Him. Doing so will result in more effective ministry and will increase your satisfaction as you serve. This kind of service is an opportunity to partner with God in changing His world.

God's Time Is Now

Open your heart. Read and digest Scripture. Include Christ in all the details of your life. Examine all that you do in the light of what you know He wants you to do. Give God all your excuses, and sing out in full obedience and volume, "Lord Jesus, I long to be perfectly whole; I want You forever to live in my soul."[2]

May your journey with God be glorious! As you embrace Him (and He embraces you), remember that no event is without His nearness and no crisis without His grace. While your pilgrimage will be unique, the important thing is that you travel with your Savior, Sustainer and Friend.

—⟶⟵—

I want to know Christ and the power of his resurrection and the fellowship of sharing in his sufferings, becoming like him in his death, and so, somehow, to attain to the resurrection from the dead.

PHILIPPIANS 3:10-11

grace

making Christ
the center

Lately, when I pray, read Scripture and listen carefully, I've really seen God's guidance and involvement in the details of ministry. I ran across this verse in Isaiah that describes exactly how I feel: "Whether you turn to the right or to the left, your ears will hear a voice behind you, saying, 'This is the way; walk in it'" (30:21).

DARYL, 29, ALASKA

Your hunger for God begins to be satisfied as you discover the unifying center for your thoughts, feelings and values. Discovering the center doesn't come from some New Age mysticism. Rather, finding the center is simple—it means embracing Christ and taking Him into the details.

Organizing All You Do
Around Christ

As your Center, Christ completes your incompleteness. He satisfies your hunger for significance. Centering on Jesus provides an inner orderliness and generates a spiritual energy that supplies vitality for all dimensions of your life and ministry. Consider the following ways that centering on Christ will make your faith functional rather than theoretical, present rather than ancient, and practical rather than ethereal.

Centering on Christ Stabilizes Life

As you allow Christ into the corners of your life, a holistic perspective begins to shape your thoughts, monitor your conversations, question your attitudes and evaluate your achievements. Like the operating system of a computer, a Christ-centered life sorts out the differences between the peripheral and the essential. The most obvious benefit is intimacy with Christ—a relationship in which He guides, motivates and resources the details of your life and ministry. While you'll still go through times when fog rolls into your life, Christ stabilizes your inner world so that you can more easily tolerate crashing seas and threatening winds.

Centering on Christ Shifts Focus from Self

Making an intentional shift to Christ-directedness from self-directedness begins when you give careful attention to the inner issues of character, motives and intentions, and give less attention to good appearances, image and impressions. Centering makes Jesus the significant point for thought, speech and action in your life and ministry. Centering redirects life around Jesus. Your stress goes down because "all things hold together" (Col. 1:17) in Him. Essentially, this intentional part of centering requires you to surrender without reservation the controlling interest of everything about yourself to Christ. With Christ in charge and not a hint of resistance from you, He shapes every dimension of life. This saves you a lot of agony and encourages authentic commitments to issues that really matter.

Centering on Christ Heals Internal Confusion

No matter how small, conflicting commitments can generate turmoil in your soul. The resulting havoc wrecks the quality of your life. However, when the Center is allowed to coordinate all facets of who you are and what you long to become, you can experience a life and ministry of amazing power, peace and confidence.

These results are abundantly possible with Christ as your Center.

Once you experience a centered life, it doesn't make any sense to go back to the old fragmented way of living. Just a simple encounter with Christ puts Him in your heart forever. Then the Father is always with you, calling you home wherever you go, whatever you do and whatever you become. This God-closeness will shape you, even when life's frustrations stress you. With Philip you can pray, "Lord, show us the Father and *that will be enough*" (John 14:8, emphasis added). And He *is* enough. A fulfilling serenity flourishes in the inner world of all who live in intimate contact with Jesus Christ.

Helps for Centering on Christ

Admittedly, placing Christ at the very center of your life isn't as easy as it sounds. But it's also not nearly as difficult as some people try to make it. The main roadblock to living a centered life is giving up your self-sovereignty. But so much lies ahead when you're willing to do that. As you've seen, centering on Christ promises radically new ways of living and serving. Here are several ways to make Christ the Center of your life and ministry.

Think Small

Bigger isn't always better. Louder isn't always more true. Look for the good to be found in ordinary days, even when they appear to be ho-hum and routine. Seek deliverance from addiction to the spectacular. Cherish the ordinary. Elijah learned that God sometimes speaks in a still, small voice (see 1 Kings 19:11-12). Spirituality doesn't need to be sensational to be supernatural.

Make a Faith Statement with Your Living

Your way of life advertises what you believe. Your choices either give credibility to your values or undermine them. What you believe affects your ministry, worship and play; and the way you serve, worship and play publicizes your values to the world. Try thinking of the truly centered life as a nonverbal headline that points others to God. Ask God to help this statement be true of you: My life is most attractive to others when I am spiritually strong enough to deal with the strains and difficulties that will inevitably come.

Practice the Presence

Acknowledging God's constant presence and companionship can immunize you against many secular preoccupations. Just knowing that God is there tunes you in to Him. Start practicing His presence by asking God's approval on the letters and e-mails you write, the phone calls you make, the conversations you share, the books you read and the TV programs you watch. The possibilities are endless.

Be Satisfied with Enough

Nearly everyone spends too much energy on concerns about money, security and ownership. No one is completely free from money stress—you don't have enough, you want more, or you work too hard just to keep what you have. God promises that He cares for even the smallest creatures, so you can safely relinquish your security hang-ups to Him. Don't allow greed to spread its seductive lies in your life or ministry. Trust God, who is faithful, extravagant and gracious.

Resist Distractions

In order to hear God more effectively, you must intentionally cultivate the capacity to listen. A truly centered life requires intentional periods of silence in order to hear Him accurately. One way to quiet distractions is to think intently about a name or attribute of Jesus. Try "Savior," "Lord," "Emmanuel" or "Redeemer." Useful attributes include love, mercy, peace and hope. Another centering technique involves meditating on the meaning of biblical words such as "faith," "patience," "meekness," "righteousness" and "sanctification." If you experience mental drifting, tell yourself, *I'll think about that later; right now I'm centering on Christ.* Then return to the name, attribute or Bible promise that you were using to help you center on Him.

Relive Jesus' Life in Your World

Reliving Jesus' life in your world involves trying to see your world through His eyes and responding as He would. What would He do in your home or office? What does He think about your relationships? What would He say about a trying situation in your ministry? You can greatly enhance your efforts to relive Christ by following Paul's directive in Philippians 4:8-9:

> Finally, brothers, whatever is true, whatever is noble, whatever is right, whatever is pure, whatever is lovely, whatever is admirable—if anything is excellent or praiseworthy—think about such things. Whatever you have learned or received or heard from me, or seen in me— put it into practice. And the God of peace will be with you.

Share Your Dreams and Your Spiritual Discoveries

Finally, your journey of faith will be strengthened when you share your hopes and dreams with a trusted, spiritually mature friend. And nothing is more powerful than giving another person the opportunity to be involved in your quest for Christlikeness. The result is that the inner flame will be fanned in two like-minded people who then can sustain and care for each other through the flat times.

—⚮—

When the kindness and love of God our Savior appeared, he saved us, not because of righteous things we had done, but because of his mercy. He saved us through the washing of rebirth and renewal by the Holy Spirit, whom he poured out on us generously through Jesus Christ our Savior, so that, having been justified by his grace, we might become heirs having the hope of eternal life.

TITUS 3:4-7

grace

embracing God
enriches your
ministry

*Last Sunday, I preached from Luke 24 about the two
defeated disciples on the Road to Emmaus. Two people
came forward and received the risen Savior into their
hearts! In many ways, I needed this message as much as
my congregation did—I'm always amazed at how God
strengthens us in our times of despair and brokenness.*

CHRIS, 55, WASHINGTON

When you embrace God and pursue Christ as the
Center of your life and ministry, you experience myri-
ad benefits. Topping the list is knowing without any
doubt that God is with you and that He is for you.

Wherever spiritual resources and ordinary life intersect, God is there—enriching your service for Christ.

Intimacy with God means experiencing God's nearness in such a way that it is vivid, real and affirming. It's as if He touches your hand and speaks an audible word. It's an awareness that despite your inadequacies, God is present to make you strong and effective. This intimacy with God is as much for you as it is for the people you serve. It provides incredible joy, remarkable strength and amazing staying power for ministry.

A Ministry of Enriched Service

Consider some of the ways that embracing God in this intimate way enriches your service for Him.

God Is Present in Active Expressions of Love

Intimacy with God means knowing that you have a Helper who comes beside you in any expression of active love that you give in Jesus' name—a sympathetic word, a caring action, a trusting prayer, a thoughtful note or a redemptive touch. It means dramatically sensing God's presence in those special heart-to-heart moments when you experience God with another person and you know that two have become three, and the third is the Son of God.

God Provides a Supernatural Connection

Embracing God intimately means having such a strong connection with Him that you can replicate the character of Jesus in your service for Him. His reliability, wholeness and faith show up in you and your ministry. This holy nearness releases extraordinary expressions of compassion, increased spiritual savvy, authentic ways of seeing, empowered ways of being, and divinely energized ways of doing. This connection means that you can take God with you into circumstances filled with chaos or painful alienation. Or better, it means that He can take you into those situations. Either way, this is an incarnational realization that Jesus is with you in ministry, and you know it. Those you serve see it, too. And in the encounters, those who lead and those who follow are amazed and grateful that this association between them is more than friendship or a mere professional relationship.

When you embrace God at this intimate level, you are so totally open to the Almighty that He shows Himself through your feeble human efforts. This intimacy helps you continue the Kingdom work that Jesus started during His earthly ministry, for He promised, "I tell you the truth, anyone who has faith in me will do what I have been doing. He will do even greater things than these" (John 14:12). Intimacy with God is an assuring awareness that as an authentic ambassador of Christ, you'll never need to carry out any facet of ministry alone.

God Empowers You for Both the Mundane and the Spectacular

Face it—delivering care and compassion sometimes takes you into the dregs of human life, where what you see or feel can be shocking, untidy, untamed and even miserable. Your call and work puts you in places where you see people at their best—and their worst. So sometimes you feel helpless and useless. And that's precisely what you are when you try to minister without God.

But *with* Him, your ministry becomes amazingly exciting work. You realize the eternal implications of what you're doing. While a situation may not seem any different when God is with you, you are different when He is near, and that makes everything else sparkle with meaning. You can have the living Christ and His power in your ministry. Jesus promised, "I tell you the truth, if you have faith and do not doubt, . . . you can say to this mountain, 'Go, throw yourself into the sea,' and it will be done. If you believe, you will receive whatever you ask for in prayer" (Matt. 21:21-22).

A World Crowded with God

Every facet of your ministry can be saturated with God. What an adventuresome partnership occurs when you embrace Him intimately! The result is that even when you try to serve in your own might with your own skills, God gloriously surprises you in unexpected places, at miraculous times and in extraordinary ways.

He becomes your Companion and your not-so-secret Source for Kingdom endeavors. He reminds you of what you already know—that no expression of service will ever be greater than its source.

At some point, every pastor must decide what or who his source will be. Will your source be ordination, authority, education, family, reputation, experience, church or Christ Himself? You have to decide whether you'll be a minister of Christ or a minister of the church. Anyone can be a minister of the church without Christ, but no one can be a genuine minister of Christ without authentically having an impact on the church.

A Christ-resourced ministry will have an incredible attraction to those you serve, even when they don't fully understand it. But they still respond. When you take Christ into the details of the ministry, you become a Christ-energized magnet to needy people. And you'll find your work more satisfying and productive.

Your call allows you the privilege of walking into people's problems uninvited and accompanied by the empowerment of God. So why go alone? When you share someone's pain in Jesus' name, you can't explain away the pain or deny the dilemma. But you can redemptively take God with you into the middle of the anguish. As God nourishes people through you, it's enough. As Christ's representative, you can simply encourage people with this message: In every part of life, God is there for you. Look up and take courage.

—⁂—

Who is wise and understanding among you? Let him show it by his good life, by deeds done in the humility that comes from wisdom.

JAMES 3:13

grace

embracing God makes your service effective

When a member of our church recently confessed to me a sin that could have destroyed his life and the future of his family, I had no answer. Yet from somewhere deep within me, the exact words needed for the situation flowed out of my mouth. Although I was totally inadequate to deal with this crisis on my own, God provided the exact answer I needed to give.

JESS, 40, VIRGINIA

Putting Christ at the center of your life and ministry not only enriches what you do but also makes you more effective. Think of how God works through you in Christian service. Maybe you make calls in the hospital with nothing more than what appears to be a few friendly words—no medicine, no scalpel, no miracle drugs and no medical credentials—but before you leave, there are encounters between God and the patients you've visited that are unique, special and eternal.

Something similar happens when you offer ministry in conversations on a beach walk, on the phone or across a restaurant table, or written in a note or an e-mail. It may soften calloused hearts. Or it may come like a gentle spring breeze.

We pastors sometimes seem to be slow learners when it comes to grasping how limited our service is when done in mere human strength and cleverness. But when a troubling crisis forces us to recognize our limitations, we can welcome God's availability, strength and empowerment.

Taking God with You

The presence of God is a unique factor you take to those you serve. Consider the following principles for taking this supernatural dynamic into pastoral care and counseling.

Never Fear God's Presence

You may have times when you want to avoid keeping close company with Jesus because of the demands He makes.

Sometimes it's easier to be interested in causes and symptoms of problems than in the cures or masteries that Jesus offers. Sometimes God wants "yes" when you prefer to say "no." Sometimes when you rush into your prayers, God reminds you, "You have been dodging Me for days." God's nearness affirms and judges you.

This searching aspect of God sounds somewhat frightening, but think of the benefits. It means that your ministry efforts are continually under His care. It means that you're never alone, never out of God's sight or hearing. God nourishes your soul, resources your ministry and puts you at ease in His presence. He wants you to take delight in the fact that He is always near. He desires your unconditional permission to walk into the details of your life and ministry. As the psalmist wrote, "Before a word is on my tongue you know it completely, O LORD. You hem me in—behind and before; you have laid your hand upon me. Such knowledge is too wonderful for me, too lofty for me to attain" (Ps. 139:4-6).

Welcome God into Pastoral Care

In ministry, God empowers you to resuscitate and reenergize people's souls. Part of your role is to present Christ as a recognized and present Person rather than as a dead hero or the ancient founder of Christianity.

You give theoretical notions about ministry a face and a heart—the face and heart of Jesus.

You represent the transcendent power of God—a power that all people reach for in times of pressing need. You present Christ to individuals and to a society in desperate need of God. This means that you must be so saturated with intimate Christ-centered living that people see Him in you. You need to desert your professional pedestal and cast your lot with the needy people of your church and community—to live out the character of Christ with them in their pain and problems, and in their victories, too.

People want God when their baby dies, when medical reports are bad, when jobs are lost, and when the unexplainable makes life desperate. In troubled times like these, people need to know that the living Lord identifies thoroughly with them; He sat where they sit, felt what they feel, and suffered what they suffer. That is why you must develop an intimate relationship with God—sometimes you're His only representative whom suffering people can actually see.

Sharpen Your Awareness of God's Presence

Although Christ is everywhere, most of us need to sharpen our awareness of His nearness. Increasing your awareness of God's presence requires you to actively welcome God into every phase of living, especially in those places where you're trying to help others in His name and at those times when you represent Him. The demands of pastoral care, counseling and soul friendship create in you the greatest need for God's presence.

Representing the Father in such settings is a privilege. He has promised to help you when you listen carefully to what He wants you to say and do. He hears your heart, and you can hear His when you've embraced Him. He answers when you pray with the psalmist,

> Look on me and answer, O LORD my God. Give light to my eyes, or I will sleep in death; my enemy will say, "I have overcome him," and my foes will rejoice when I fall. But I trust in your unfailing love; my heart rejoices in your salvation. I will sing to the LORD, for he has been good to me (Ps. 13:3-6).

Cultivate Your Relationship with God to Revitalize Ministry

It's easy for life and ministry to get out of focus. Some days, it seems that hundreds of voices—including your own—are calling for your attention and help.

However, your intimate relationship with Christ will keep you and your church on track. You must continually remind yourself that you battle with weapons that are essentially spiritual and supernatural. The apostle Paul put this in clear perspective:

> The weapons we fight with are not the weapons of the world. On the contrary, they have divine power to demolish strongholds. We demolish arguments and every pretension that sets itself up against the knowledge of God, and we take captive every thought to make it obedient to Christ (2 Cor. 10:4-5).

Only by embracing God can you look past the problems to seize the possibilities of a Christ-shaped life.

Allow God to Help You Overcome Your Hesitations

Sometimes, you just want to take a break, to put everything on hold. Of course, God provides times when you can recharge your spiritual batteries. But He also calls you to move forward in spite of how complicated your world becomes or even though you fear failure on your watch. The problem with hesitancy is that it can eventually shut down ministry completely. We heard of one Christian leader who said, "I don't want to make a mistake, so I'm overly cautious." When hesitations continue for months and years, you need to consider the potentially harmful results. If you do nothing, you'll accomplish nothing, and that undermines all the might-have-beens.

Taking God with you into ministry—or more appropriately, allowing Him to lead you into ministry—helps you know where to go, what to say, and how to say it. Give up your hesitations about changing your world, and get on with making a difference for Christ. Here's an action checklist:

- Preach what the Bible really says.
- Become a radical Christian in civic issues.
- Evangelize every class of people.
- Lead your church to live by biblical principles.
- Relinquish your painful past.
- Cultivate a soul friend or mentor.
- Care for your own soul.
- Share faith with everyone, including professionals.
- Lead in absolute dependence on God.

Intentionally Look for Christ in People You Serve

Every relationship offers an opportunity to see God—as you recognize the spiritual potential of every human being you meet. Jesus promised, "I tell you the truth, whatever you did for one of the least of these brothers of mine, you did for me" (Matt. 25:40).

Looking for God in everyone you serve takes the dread out of ministry and even transforms ministry into an adventure. Try it as you start your day tomorrow. See the face of Christ in every person you meet, and see every problem person as a potential saint. Feel every heartache. Then your duties will be transformed into delights of service offered in Jesus' name to the people He loves.

Expect God to Help You Make the Ordinary Significant

Intimacy with Christ can also keep you faithful at hard tasks in ordinary places. On a human basis, you probably have at least 10 good reasons—or maybe 100—for why you should quit. Some longtime pastors say that they have many good reasons to resign every Sunday! However, every place is worthy of a leader who dreams big dreams for the Kingdom in that setting.

The testimony of the spiritual giants in every century is that they always found enough light and enough energy for the next step. They reported that God is always on time—but seldom ahead of time. They unanimously state that beyond coincidence and well beyond their reasoning, they found a Guide, a Companion, a Source and a Confidant. God made it possible for them to accomplish great exploits for Him. Their achievements were based on their partnership with God. Their victories often followed their defeats.

Even now, you may be bewildered about where God has placed you to serve Him. Remember, God is never confused about you or your situation. One of God's delightfully amazing surprises is to transform all your liabilities—whether social, familial or economic—into incredible good for His kingdom. God isn't baffled by your needs or inexperience. Allow Him to use you and make the humdrum exciting right where you are until He moves you.

The Powerful Presence

What benefit does embracing God intimately give your life and ministry? Certainly not immunity to pain, brokenness or adversaries. Throughout all human history, Christian service has always involved God's call to come and die for the gospel. What a unique call!

Instead, intimacy with God is an active awareness that works in partnership with the living Christ. It's a sense of standing in Christ's place, calling persons to miraculous reconciliation with God, themselves and others.

In the presence of the King, your work is better, every system of your body and brain is at full attention, and you desire to please Him. Your efforts, then, are more intensely motivated to distinctive service for Him.

—⁓—

The Spirit himself testifies with our spirit that we are God's children. Now if we are children, then we are heirs—heirs of God and co-heirs with Christ, if indeed we share in his sufferings in order that we may also share in his glory.

ROMANS 8:16-17

grace

the next
step

Ministry today is more difficult than it's ever been. Each day, it seems that we hear of another colleague who has fallen into immorality, another who has burned out, another who has in some way weakened the credibility of those called to God's ministry.

What's happening? Perhaps the hectic expectations we encounter in ministry cause us to lose sight of the commitments we made when we first accepted Christ as our Lord and Savior. Perhaps the standards we promised to live by when we followed His call to be His ministers have been overshadowed by exhaustion or carelessness. Whatever the cause, men and women in ministry are increasingly facing a crisis of integrity, righteousness and credibility.

What would it take for each of us to commit ourselves to a lifestyle more pleasing to the Lord, to our congregations, to our families and to ourselves? What would it look like if today's pastors arose to truly lead the church, to authentically serve as examples to our congregations and to faithfully represent Christ to the world? What would it take to stop pastors from falling to the temptations of immorality and destroying our credibility and integrity through reckless and ill-advised behavior? What would it look like to count the cost of our actions and respond to God's prompting to avoid the traps and stumbling blocks that the enemy places in our path?

Maybe it would take a simple but sincere commitment—a call to arms. We began this book with the words to the Shepherd's Covenant. Closing the book with the same words seems appropriate—as a call to arms for all of us!

We are joined together by a common call of God to feed His sheep, but we are also tied by a common commitment to purity, holiness, righteousness and faithfulness. Our agreement to submit to the Shepherd's Covenant transcends theological differences, denominational connections and local congregational constraints. We are bound to one another by our calls, mutual accountability, and by the knowledge that one day the Great Shepherd will be our final Judge.

We further believe that when clergy are more focused on mission than on profession, we will see a renewed interest in the churches we serve and a genuine acceptance by those we seek to influence. It is through God's grace that commitment to this covenant is made possible.

Both this call to commitment and the words of this book come from our hearts and our years of experience and interaction with thousands of pastors. Over time, we've changed with you, but our resolve to serve you has not. We believe that you're a leader in the greatest movement ever known—the Church of Jesus Christ. We salute you for your courage, concern ourselves about your schedules and pray earnestly for your families.

There are times when we think, *Wouldn't it be fun to turn back the clock and assume the role of a pastor again?* Well, those days are probably gone for good, but the memories remain, and the thrill of the call will never leave us. Now the Church is in your hands—to nurture, protect and guide. Eternity will record the fruit of your labor.

He tends his flock like a shepherd: He gathers the lambs in his arms and carries them close to his heart (Isa. 40:11).

Carry on, colleague, carry on.

H. B. and Neil

———⟋⟍⟍⟍⟋———

The Shepherd's Covenant represents a growing movement that calls pastors to commit to a new level of accountability and devotion to the call of God on their lives. For more information about making this commitment to God, your family, your congregation and your fellow pastors, write to this address:

Pastoral Ministries
c/o Focus on the Family
P.O. Box 35500
Colorado Springs, CO 80935

Or visit us online at www.parsonage.org, and click on the Shepherd's Covenant link.

ACKNOWLEDGMENTS

Each new book becomes a labor of love. *The Shepherd's Covenant for Pastors* was no exception.

Our thanks to Kim Bangs, Deena Davis and all the great folks at Regal Books, who keep on having faith in us;

to our editor, Brad Lewis, who makes the pages sing;

to a special couple, Jim and Judy DeVries, who from the beginning supported H. B.'s dream for the covenant;

and to the dedicated pastoral ministry staff at Focus on the Family—Gary, Roger, Dan, John, Alex, Ralph, George, Jan, Julie, Kathy, Eunice, Teresa and H. B.'s assistant for the past 33 years, Sue McFadden;

and most of all, to all of you shepherds, who have proven to be our inspiration.

ENDNOTES

Preface

1. Julia H. Johnston, "Grace Greater than Our Sin," quoted in *The Celebration Hymnal* (n.p.: Word Music and Integrity Music, 1997), song no. 344.

Introduction

1. William Barclay, *The Mind of St. Paul* (New York: Harper, 1958), p. 169.
2. Forrest Church, ed., *Restoring Faith* (New York: Walker and Company, 2001), p. 133.
3. Whitney J. Dough, ed., *Sayings of E. Stanley Jones* (Franklin, TN: Providence House Publishers, 1994), p. 71.
4. Isaac Watts, "When I Survey the Wondrous Cross," quoted in *The Celebration Hymnal* (n.p.: Word Music and Integrity Music, 1997), song no. 324.

Chapter 2

1. The Barna Group, "Americans Are Most Likely to Base Truth on Feelings," *The Barna Update*, February 12, 2002. http://www.barna.org/FlexPage.aspx?Page=BarnaUpdate&BarnaUpdateID=106 (accessed March 24, 2005).

Chapter 4

1. Charles Swindoll, quoted in Chuck Colson, *The Body: Being Light in Darkness* (Dallas, TX: Word, 1992), p. 131.
2. Rick Warren, quoted in C. Peter Wagner, *Prayer Shield* (Ventura, CA: Regal Books, 1992), pp. 194-195.

Chapter 9

1. James Bright, quoted in Edward S. Mann, *Linked to a Cause* (Kansas City, MO: Pedestal Press, 1986), n.p.
2. *Merriam-Webster's Collegiate Dictionary,* 11th ed., s.v. "pastor."
3. John W. Frye, *Jesus the Pastor* (Grand Rapids, MI: Zondervan Publishing House, 2000), p. 48.

Chapter 14

1. Archibald D. Hart, "Being Moral Isn't Always Enough," *Leadership,* vol. 9, no. 2 (Spring 1988), p. 29.

Chapter 15

1. Ted Engstrom, *The Makings of a Christian Leader* (Grand Rapids, MI: Fleming H. Revell, 1986), p. 117.

Chapter 17

1. John Benson, quoted in an article in *Herald of Holiness,* a magazine published by the General Board of the Church of the Nazarene, Kansas City, MO.
2. James L. Nicholson, "Whiter than Snow," quoted in *The Celebration Hymnal* (n.p.: Word Music and Integrity Music, 1997), song no. 653.

for pastors and
churches

Pastoral Resources and Services Available from the Pastoral Ministries Department of Focus on the Family

The resources listed in this section are available by calling 1-800-A-FAMILY or visiting www.parsonage.org.

Website

The Parsonage (www.parsonage.org)—a home page for ministers and their families.

Toll-Free Phone Line

The Clergy Care Line (1-877-233-4455)—a listening ear or word of advice from our staff of pastors for ministers, missionaries, chaplains and their families.

Audiocassettes and Compact Discs

Pastor to Pastor—a series of audiocassettes or CDs, available as a bimonthly subscription or individual sets. Features H. B. London interviewing Christian experts on topics pertaining to the personal and family lives of pastors, such as pastors in crisis, keeping romance alive, overcoming weariness, retaining your own identity as a pastor's wife, dangers of the Internet, and pastors as parents.

Newsletter

The Pastor's Weekly Briefing—a quick look at current events of interest to pastors, their families and their congregations. Available by e-mail or at the website.

Congregational Booklets

The Pastor's Advocate Series—a set of booklets designed to help congregations better understand pastors and their families, better care for them and better join them in ministry.

Resource Directory

The Pastoral Care Directory—an invaluable list of ministries specializing in care for pastoral families, plus the best in books, audiocassettes, videos, publications and other resources (available both in print and online).

Books by the Authors

London, H. B., Jr. *Refresh, Renew, Revive: How to Encourage Your Spirit, Strengthen Your Family, and Energize Your Ministry.* Colorado Springs, CO: Focus on the Family, 1996.

London, H. B., Jr., and Neil B. Wiseman. *Becoming Your Favorite Church.* Ventura, CA: Regal Books, 2002.

———. *For Kids' Sake.* Ventura, CA: Regal Books, 2004.

———. *The Heart of a Great Pastor: How to Grow Strong and Thrive Wherever God Has Planted You.* Ventura, CA: Regal Books, 1994.

———. *Married to a Pastor: How to Stay Happily Married in the Ministry.* Ventura, CA: Regal Books, 1999.

———. *Pastors at Greater Risk.* Ventura, CA: Regal Books, 2003.

———. *They Call Me Pastor: How to Love the Ones You Lead.* Ventura, CA: Regal Books, 2000.

Wiseman, Neil B. *Come to the Water Brook.* Kansas City, MO: Beacon Hill Press, 1997.

———. *Conditioning Your Soul.* Kansas City, MO: Beacon Hill Press, 1999.

————. *Hunger for the Holy—71 Ways to Get Closer to God.* Grand Rapids, MI: Baker Books, 1996.

————. *Maximizing Your Church's Spiritual Potential.* Kansas City, MO: Beacon Hill Press, 1999.

————. *The Untamed God—Unleashing the Supernatural in the Body of Christ.* Kansas City, MO: Beacon Hill Press, 1996.

Pastor Conferences and Seminars

H. B. London and Neil B. Wiseman are available to speak at conferences, conventions and organizations concerning the ideas described in this book, pastoral renewal, the inner life of the Christian and the renewal of the supernatural in the Body of Christ. Wiseman, who has led the Small Church Institute since 1991, also does consulting with denominational leaders concerning issues facing smaller congregations.

Internet Contact Information

H. B. London: http://www.parsonage.org

Neil B. Wiseman: nbwiseman@aol.com